Depression and Suicide in Children and Adolescents

Prevention, Intervention, and Postvention

PHILIP G. PATROS

Southern Connecticut State University

TONIA K. SHAMOO

Bristol Public Schools—Bristol, Connecticut
Southern Connecticut State University

ALLYN AND BACON, INC.
Boston London Sydney Toronto

121639

Library of Congress Cataloging-in-Publication Data

Patros, Philip G.
    Depression and suicide in children and adolescents: prevention,
intervention, and postvention Philip G. Patros, Tonia K. Shamoo.
        p. cm.
    Bibliography: p.
    Includes index.
    ISBN 0-205-11670-1
    1. Children—United States—Suicidal behavior.   2. Teenagers—
United States—Suicidal behavior.   3. Suicide—United States—
Prevention.   4. Depression in children.   I. Shamoo, Tonia K.
II. Title.
HV6546.P38 1988
362.2—dc19   88-14448
                                                                     CIP

Printed in the United States of America
10 9 8 7 6 5 4 3 2 1 92 91 90 89 88

This book is dedicated with abounding love and honor to my nephew and godson,

Thomas J. Massad,

who passed away with faith, respect, and dignity on September 25, 1987.

He would have gladly traded his painful, incurable cancer for the discomforts, pain, and frustrations of life that some people feel are reasons for suicide.

His valiant struggle for survival and the ways he appreciated and loved life should inspire all of us to help those who believe that suicide is the only answer.

Philip G. Patros

Contents

Preface

Despite the dramatic increase in the suicidal behavior of children and adolescents, research in the field has been neglected and controversial. Although the increase for suicide in the age ranges of fifteen to twenty-four years has been documented, there are few reliable statistics for children, ages four to fourteen years, who take their lives. This may be partly due to the refusal of parents and authorities to believe that children can and do kill themselves. It is also possible that some deaths attributed to accidents are, in reality, suicides. Social, legal, and religious restraints often make it difficult to distinguish between accidents and suicide attempts. Families, and the children themselves, hide suicide attempts for a variety of reasons. Parents may be afraid of being disgraced or of what other people think, and may not take the suicide attempt seriously. Very often injuries from suicidal attempts are not perceived as such.

It is estimated that thousands of children are admitted to hospitals each year for suicide attempts. However, we feel that this respresents only a small percent of those who have tried self-destructive behaviors. In our private practice, we have seen an increase in children with self-destructive tendencies and/or behaviors. Presently within the schools more depressed and suicidal children and adolescents are coming to the attention of teachers, school social workers, school psychologists, and counselors. It is more likely for children to make an attempt to commit suicide, without intending to

complete the act, than to succeed. If these children go unrecognized, the risk increases for subsequent attempts and
completion. Therefore, early detection and intervention at
the school level becomes strategically important.

Due to our workshops and contacts in schools, we have
become aware of the increased stresses put on children and
the increased concern by students and faculty alike of self-
destructive behaviors. Information about suicide, like information about sex, is not being given to students due to the
fear that knowledge of the subject will increase the likeli-
hood of it occurring. This is in contrast to the school's role
and purpose of teaching and providing knowledge. Students
express great concerns about suicidal behaviors and suicide,
especially after a suicide has occurred in the school or community. They turn to staff members for information and understanding, but all to often there is a lack of accurate
information and guidelines.

Staff members have also expressed their concerns about
suicide. They often see behaviors and/or hear statements that
reflect a student's suicidal intention, yet it is seldom recognized in the context of suicide, and all too often the clues are
ignored. This is not because of lack of caring but of not
knowing what to do. Many times, there is no prescribed approach to dealing with such students on a school-wide or
system-wide basis, and even special service personnel are
often at a loss in how to deal with these issues. Suicide, like
other significant student-related issues, needs to be addressed on a system-wide basis, giving educators and students appropriate guidelines to follow that will enhance
knowledge and facilitate intervention.

Prevention is probably the most significant aspect of any
system-based program. There must be adequately trained
staff and facilities to address the concerns and needs of all
age-level students. It is imperative that counselors, school social workers, and school psychologists have a firm foundation of knowledge of the varied causes and underlying
themes of these self-destructive behaviors. They must recognize the signals of self-destructive behaviors and, most im-

portantly, they must have the skills necessary to work with these troubled children.

It is this awareness and concern that has led us to the writing of this book.

Section One is an overview of child and adolescent suicide, family patterns seen in suicidal children and adolescents, and how children and adolescents view death. This section also deals with depression and the manifestation of depression in the general context of suicide.

Section Two presents information that will aid school personnel in recognizing situational, behavioral, and feeling signals of depression and suicidal behavior. In addition, myths and misinformation about suicide will be discussed, and sources of student stress in school and in the classroom will be presented.

Section Three provides suicide prevention, intervention, and postvention guidelines. Intervention techniques are also suggested to aid those professionals who come into contact and need to work with low-risk suicidal children.

The various case studies interspersed throughout the book are composites of actual cases, changed to insure the confidentiality of the students and their families.

It is our hope that this book will fulfill a need for schools and school systems in developing a program for dealing with students who are depressed and suicidal.

Section One

Section One provides the background that is necessary for a clear understanding of suicidal behaviors. This section is an overview of child and adolescent suicides, depression, family patterns, and child and adolescent perceptions of death.

CHAPTER 1

Overview

CHILDREN'S SUICIDE

Various theoretical issues contribute to the sparsity of available data on children's (ages one to twelve years old) suicide and the collection of statistics. Several issues and problems in the fields of child psychology and child development reflect today's concerns with childhood depression: (1) children younger than ten years of age do not have a concept of the finality of death; (2) completed suicide among children is rare (Shaffer, 1974); (3) children do not have the physical prowess to effect a fatal self-injury (Gould, 1965); and (4) there is a lack of standard diagnostic techniques for suicide assessment.

Although Garfinkel, Froese, and Hood (1982) imply that children use suicidal behaviors to draw attention to their conflicts, many professionals believe that children are incapable of suicidal behavior. Gould (1965), for example, postulates that children, because of their size, strength, motor coordination, and access to needed material, are unable to plan and execute a suicide. These beliefs are slowly being disproved as researchers begin to substantiate suicidal behaviors in children. Turkington (1983, p. 13) suggests that children are more likely to "attempt suicide without intending to complete it, than to succeed."

These issues have partially influenced the collection and classification of vital statistics for suicidal behavior of children. Although information based on analysis of mortality data indicates that suicide is the tenth leading cause of death in children ages one to fourteen years, it is felt that this is an understatement of the true number of suicides (Center for Disease Control, 1985). This is partially due to the incredulity of parents and authorities that children can and do kill themselves. The underestimation of suicide rates in children may be related to the number of deaths reported as accidental. (Accidents are the leading cause of death among young children.) In addition, various social, legal, and religious restraints may limit the accurate reporting and postmortem assessment of the causes of death (Pfeffer, 1981).

Researchers indicate that the threat of suicide is the reason for referral to child clinics of 8 to 10% of the patients admitted (Lukianowicz, 1968; Mattson, Seese, and Hawkins, 1969). Also, Cohen-Sandler, Berman, and King (1982) suggest that about 12,000 children, ages five to fourteen years, are admitted annually to psychiatric hospitals for suicidal behaviors.

Clinical studies have highlighted the variety of techniques that children use for their self-destructive acts. Methods such as toxin ingestion, hanging, jumping from heights, running into traffic, and cutting or stabbing have been documented (Ackerly, 1967; Lukianowicz, 1968; Pfeffer et al., 1979). Cohen-Sandler, Berman, and King (1982) report that children over age nine are more likely to take medication, toxic or nontoxic materials (such as roach spray), rubbing alcohol, or even turtle food, whereas younger children are more likely to jump from buildings or run into traffic.

Orbach, Gross, and Glaubman (1981) identify four dimensions that they feel describe suicidal behaviors in young children: (1) the attractiveness of life, which refers to the degree to which life is attractive and enjoyable; (2) the repulsiveness of life, which is composed of experience of mental and physical suffering; (3) the attractiveness of death, consisting of various cultural and religious beliefs about death; and (4) the repulsiveness of death, referring to the degree to which death arouses fear and anxiety.

Suicidal behavior of children is a complex symptom that is influenced by the interactive effects of environmental, developmental, and intrapsychic factors. Thus, an evaluation of the degree of suicidal risk of children must include a systematic assessment of these variables. The relative significance of each factor may differ with the individual child. Nevertheless, the primary and immediate concern ought to be the guaranteed safety of the child. Only then should an intensive evaluation of the underlying problem and intervention be carried out (Pfeffer, 1981).

If nonfatal suicidal attempts are left unrecognized and untreated, the risk increases for subsequent attempts and completion (Cohen-Sandler and Berman, 1980). Therefore, early detection and intervention become strategically important (Garfinkel and Golombek, 1974).

ADOLESCENTS' SUICIDE

In the past twenty years the suicide rate for adolescents has drastically increased, whereas the overall suicide rate for the nation has remained fairly stable. Over 1,000 teenagers a day attempt suicide; estimates indicate that 18 of these adolescents succeed on a daily basis. This translates to 57 attempts every hour; approximately every hour and a half, one of our young people takes his or her life. There is speculation that suicidal attempts have risen as much as 3,000% a year (Select Committee on Aging, House of Representatives, 1985).

Adolescents (ages thirteen to twenty-two years old) use a variety of methods to attempt suicide. Since it is frequently an impulsive act, they will often use whatever means are available. It is generally felt that girls will use a method of lower immediate lethality than boys. This would explain why the rate of completed suicides is higher for adolescent boys than girls (a 5:1 ratio), since there is less time for intervention by others (Center for Disease Control, 1986). Most child and adolescent suicide attempts are made in the home, which suggests that intervention is a possibility.

The Center for Disease Control (1985) has reported an interesting overall trend for females: The pattern of suicide by method for females, of all ages, has had a significant change between 1970 and 1980, whereas the pattern for males has remained the same. The leading method of suicide for males has consistently been firearms. In 1970, the leading method of suicide for females was poisoning by solids or liquids, followed by firearms. In 1980, there was a reversal in the trend for females; the leading method became firearms, followed by poisoning. Some of the more commonly used methods are guns (40.0%), hanging (20.0%), drugs (17.5%), carbon monoxide (7.3%), jumping (7.2%), and drownings (2.4%). The peak times for youth suicide appears to be late fall and early winter, contrasting with the adults' peak time of spring. It has also been reported by Baron (1986) that 23% of suicides occur just before or after a victim's birthday.

Ray and Johnson (1983) state that the most prevalent causes of adolescent suicide are depression, loss of parent, and alienation from the family. Depression in adolescents may stem from a wide range of situations that involve social interactions such as failure, loss of love object, rejection, and so on, but in some cases depression can also be caused by biochemical imbalances (Hipple and Cimbolic, 1979).

Some adolescents have great difficulty in adjusting to the actual or felt loss of a parent. Upon such a loss, some adolescents feel rejected, which in turn leads to feelings of guilt and worthlessness. Loss of a parent removes or displaces the role model for many developing young people, which is a major factor in behavioral patterns (Finch and Pozaznski, 1971; McAnarney, 1979). The reasons for alienation from the family are numerous and when family closeness and communication are undermined suicide rates seem to rise.

Alcohol and drugs are closely related to suicide because they tend to reduce anxiety and psychological pain. There is a reduction of inhibitions, which allows the adolescent to express more easily his or her anger and unhappiness through suicidal behavior. Alcohol and drugs also allow suicidal impulses to be magnified, thus increasing the risk. The use of alcohol and drugs provides adolescents with a temporary and false security in dealing with their problems. Unfortunately, unless these individuals learn new and effective ways of dealing with their problems, suicide may become a more viable option.

There are, of course, other factors that affect adolescent suicide, such as living in a highly mobile society that prevents the establishing of stable roots, having difficulty establishing an identity as to sex role, perceiving the need to succeed and the fear of failure, feeling the pressure to grow up too soon, and experiencing the stresses and demands placed on an adolescent by family, peers, and school. This is by no means an exhaustive list, but it indicates that the reasons for suicide are endless.

Experience has shown that those individuals who attempt suicide give warning signs, some of which are obvious and some that even a trained professional would have trouble identifying. These warning signs, which will be discussed further in Chapter 8, are verbal, behavioral, and/or situational. There are also behavior patterns or syndromes, such as depression, that are viewed as warnings that suicide may be contemplated.

CERTIFICATION OF SUICIDE

As with the collection of statistics for children who kill themselves, there is also a lack of reliable data for teens. Reasons for this may be due to a lack of standardized criteria for classifying whether a death is a suicide or not, or there may be inadequate information to determine the cause of a death. Without a note that the death was self-inflicted, a death might be viewed as a homicide, an accident, or undetermined. Adolescent suicide notes are uncommon. Shaffer (1974) found that less than half of those who died left notes, whereas other researchers feel that only a very small number (about 3 to 5%) leave notes.

Another difficulty in certifying a death as a suicide is error in judgment or bias on the part of the person certifying the death (Center for Disease Control, 1985). Error in judgment may be due to an unwillingness of the family and/or physician to impart information to the examiner concerning the family and/or victim, resulting in misrepresentation of the death. With ill-defined standards or criteria for determining a death as a suicide, two examiners or certifiers using the same information may make different judgments as to whether a death is a suicide or not. Bias may occur when pressure is brought upon the certifier to avoid stigmatizing the family or victim.

In a briefing on suicide and suicide prevention for the House of Representatives' subcommittee on human services of the select committee on aging (1985), it was reported that in some states if a suicide note is not found then the death is not ruled a suicide. In another state, if a person is found hung and there are scratches around the neck and skin underneath the fingernails then the death is not judged to be a suicide. The reasoning for this conclusion is that the person changed his or her mind and tried to stop the death.

Contributing to the data collection confusion are our social and cultural influences. Due to the taboo of suicide, many deaths are recorded as accidental in order to spare the family embarrassment, humiliation, and stigmatization. If a person dies hours, days, or even weeks after a suicide attempt then the cause of death might be officially listed, for example, as "death due to complications of surgery following gunshot wound to the head." For teens, death from auto accidents, substance abuse, or eating disorders could all be possible suicides.

SUICIDE CLUSTERS

Suicide clusters are groups of deaths that are closely related in time and space. To the media, a suicide cluster can be as few as two. Rosenberg, of the Center for Disease Control, suggests that a cluster is any series of three or more deaths (Coleman, 1986).

Suicide clusters are not a new phenomenon. Probably the first recorded suicide cluster occurred around 1774 and was attributed and commented on by Johann Wolfgang von Goethe. Goethe authored *The Sorrow of Young Werther,* in which the hero committed suicide. The popular European novel was considered responsible for increased suicides (Coleman, 1986).

Two hundred years later, Phillips (1974) found that there was a significant increase in the suicide rate after a suicide made front page news. Phillips called this occurrence "the Werther effect," after Goethe's hero, and surmised that suggestion may influence and cause an increase in suicide rates. In examining suicide statistics in correlation with thirty-three publicized suicides, Phillips found that the national suicide rate increased after twenty-six of the publicized occurrences.

Phillips and Carstensen (1986) examined the relationship between nationally televised news or feature stories about suicide from 1973 to 1979 and the fluctuation in the suicide rate among American teenagers before and after the broadcasts. They found that the observed number of suicides by teenagers from zero to seven days after these televised broadcasts was significantly greater than expected. The more networks that carried the story, the greater was the increase in the suicides. Although there appears to be significant increase due to television coverage, a causal relationship cannot be clearly drawn between these broadcasts and suicides. There is no way of knowing if the adolescents who took their lives had seen the broadcasts and/or if there was a positive effect on other adolescents who had seen the broadcasts— that is, a prevention of suicide.

Coleman (1987) reports on adolescent suicide clusters for 1983 through 1986. It was found that most suicide clusters occurred in February. For individual suicides, November is the peak month for the age ranges of fifteen to twenty-nine years, whereas May is the peak month for the general population.

FACTORS OF CHILDREN
AND ADOLESCENTS AT RISK

Identifying those children and adolescents who are considered to be at high risk for suicide remains a difficult task. The study of suicide and suicidal behaviors in children and adolescents is relatively new. Literature in the area indicates that a longitudinal perspective of a child's history and life stresses, along with a clinical interview, may be the most useful in improving our predictive capabilities (Cohen-Sandler and Berman, 1982).

Core factors in the determination of suicidal behavior in children and adolescents appear to be a loss of a love object before age twelve, a dysfunctional family pattern that results in inappropriate coping skills, and ineffective communication patterns. Also, suicidal children and adolescents experience significantly greater stress than their peers. Their suicidal behavior may be the culmination of stresses that combine with the above mentioned factors.

Shneidman (1987) reports ten characteristics that he believes are common to people who commit suicide. It is our feeling that these are as applicable to youth as they are to adults. These ten characteristics are:

1. Unendurable psychological pain (an emotional pain that is so intense as to seem never ending)
2. Frustrated psychological needs (the need for security, achievement, trust, and friendship)
3. Search for a solution (suicide becomes a way out of a problem)
4. An attempt to end consciousness (stopping the awareness of pain)
5. Helplessness and hopelessness (a sense of powerlessness and impotence in dealing with pain)
6. Constriction of options (only two options are seen—a total solution or a total cessation)
7. Ambivalence (wanting to live and to die)

8. Communication of intent (clues are given about suicidal intent)
9. Departure (an ultimate run away)
10. Life-long coping patterns (the way the person endures psychological pain and uses a type of thinking that is an "either/or" pattern)

SUMMARY

Suicidal behavior is a distress signal. Researchers agree that it is more likely for children and adolescents to make an attempt to commit suicide, without intending to complete the act, than to succeed. The child and/or teen feels driven to a desperate act to call attention to problems that may have been overlooked or thought to be trivial by others. Signs almost always occur, but many times these signals go unheeded. Admittedly, it is difficult to note in a broad population specific forewarnings that would lead one to suspect that a particular child or teen may be considering suicide. However, signals are almost always given prior to a suicide attempt and may be very specific, such as making a will or giving away possessions. Other signals may not be as specific, such as changes in eating and/or sleeping habits, inability to concentrate, abrupt changes in personality, impulsiveness, slackening interest in school work, decline in grades, absenteeism, loss or lack of friends, and, for older children, alcohol and drug abuse.

Suicidal behavior in children and adolescents is fast becoming America's number one mental health problem. Depression, once thought to be nonexistent in children, is now prevalent and appears to be an underlying factor in child and adolescent suicidal behavior and suicides.

Educating parents and school personnel should be the first step to prevention and intervention. Ways to facilitate this process are to provide in-service training for school personnel on how to identify children and adolescents who are depressed and need help; educate students and set up a peer network with clear guidelines; teach children and adolescents cognitive coping skills and how to deal with stress and depression; and educate parents and school personnel through workshops as to the signals that youths might be sending. Techniques utilizing these ideas will be discussed in more detail in later chapters of the book.

CHAPTER 2

Depression

The most common impetus to suicide is depression (Friedman et al., 1984). However, some mental health professionals believe depression in very young children is nonexistent, for depression is a consequence of superego functioning, and children's superegos are not well-developed (Rochlin, 1959). It has only been in the recent, third edition of the *American Psychiatric Association's Diagnostic and Statistical Manual DSM-III* (1980) that child and adolescent depression has been listed as a diagnostic entity. It should be noted, however, that the *DSM-III* (American Psychiatric Association, 1980) utilizes adult criteria for diagnosing a major depressive disorder in children.

The *DSM-III* (American Psychiatric Association, 1980) lists the following criteria for a major depressive episode:

1. There is a loss of interest or pleasure in the usual activities, which is evidenced in the symptoms of being sad, blue, hopeless, or irritable.
2. Changes in appetite and/or weight patterns occur.
3. Sleeping patterns are altered.
4. Psychomotor agitation will increase; that is, fidgety, restless behaviors.

5. There is a loss of energy; a listlessness.
6. Self-reproach or excessive or inappropriate guilt may be apparent. (The child blames himself or herself for everything that goes wrong in his or her world.)
7. The child may be unable to concentrate and a drop in school performance may occur.
8. There may be recurrent thoughts of death or suicide.

Four of these symptoms must be present nearly every day for at least two weeks, and for those children under age six, at least three of the first four criteria will be exhibited. Also, in prepubertal children, separation anxiety may develop and cause the child to cling, to refuse to go to school, and to fear that he or she or the parents will die.

SYNDROME AND SYMPTOM

A dichotomy of views exists on the subject of childhood depression, syndrome versus symptom (Kovacs and Beck, 1977). Whereas *symptom* is a specific manifestation of behavior, *syndrome* is a configuration of behavioral symptoms that occur together (American Psychiatric Association, 1984). In order to understand these two perspectives of childhood depression, it is necessary to distinguish between them. Depression as a diagnostic syndrome includes more than just depressive feelings. It is an internal perspective on life, an attitude, a physical well-being. There is an internal sadness that prevails. When used in this context, the criteria for diagnosing depression is more restrictive, and the implications for prognosis and treatment are more specific (Emde, Harmon, and Good, 1986).

Sadness or a depressed feeling has occurred in all people at one time or another. It is a single symptom that does not necessarily suggest pathology. Emde, Harmon, and Good (1986) indicate that when a single symptom occurs, such as feeling sad or withdrawn, the general response to these depressive feelings should be viewed before it is classified as depression. Depression in infancy, preschool, school age, and adolescence have differing but overlapping characteristics.

More importantly, when considering the syndrome versus symptom perspectives, it is interesting to question if these two terms are being used to describe the same occurrences. Some professionals believe that an application of the adult diagnostic criteria as specified by DSM-III (American Psychiatric Association, 1980) is valid for children, yet there are others who believe that age-specific criteria are important. Therefore, depending on which perspective is utilized, the question remains: As children grow older, is it the way they experience depressive feelings that changes, or is it their abilities to express their depressive feelings that change?

Syndrome Perspective

Advocates of the syndrome perspective suggest that depression does occur in childhood (Bowlby, 1960; Chapman, 1974; Pearce, 1977) and that child and adult depressions are similar. It is suggested that there is an actual sadness within the child just as there is within the adult. Advocates would further argue that depressed children experience low self-esteem, irritability, weepiness, poor school performance, hopelessness, sleep and/or eating disturbances, fatigue, somatic complaints, increased aggressiveness, and involuntary urination (enuresis) or defecation (encopresis).

Although there has been a paucity of information concerning depressive disorders in early childhood, there is a growing realization along with expanding research that depression does exist in infancy and preschool age children. One of the earlier and best known studies is Spitz's (1946) description of "anaclitic depression." Spitz felt that anaclitic depression was a syndrome that resulted from the loss of a mother figure in institutionalized children who are six to twelve months of age.

CASE HISTORY
A DEPRESSED CHILD

Tom is a nine-year-old fourth grader. His parents are divorced and he lives with his mother. Visits with his father are on a regular, consistent basis and there is frequent contact between his parents concerning his schooling, discipline, and so on.

Tom had recently been dismissed from a learning disabilities resource room. He was brought to a psychologist by his parents because of behavioral difficulties, such as running away from home, destroying property, stealing from his mother, and getting in fights in school.

At the time the psychologist saw Tom his behavior had changed. He had become more subdued and withdrawn from friends. School work was not completed and his grades began to reflect this. At home Tom began to sleep on the floor, either outside his mother's bedroom door or next to her bed. He would miss his school bus in the mornings, and upon his return home would make frequent phone calls and demands to his mother at work. He began to whine and make impossible requests to both his mother and father. During this period, his beloved cat died. Tom's stomachaches and headaches increased and he was a frequent visitor to the school's health aide. He confided to the psychologist that he always felt sad and alone.

The culmination of these behaviors occurred when Tom's mother was busy preparing supper. Tom took a knife from the kitchen, destroyed a plant of his mother's, and then tried to cut himself on both wrists. Injuries were severe enough to warrant a visit to the hospital's emergency room.

Symptom Perspective

The symptom perspective holds that children cannot experience a long duration of depression and that depression is more a condition of childhood development that will disappear with time (Sheperd, Oppenheim, and Mitchell, 1971; McCaffrey, 1974). It is Anthony's view (1975) that children are susceptible to external influences, and therefore their depressive reactions tend to be more transient. Age-appropriate development in the child's cognitive, emotional, and social areas may make expression of depressive symptoms different than that of an adult.

There has been little published concerning longitudinal studies of depressed children. Determining if childhood depression is merely a transient state is impossible. It is difficult to ascertain what the duration of the episode will be, or if depression is a primary or secondary disorder (i.e., is depression causing anorexia or is the anorexia causing depression?). Also, it is thought-provoking to question if children grow up to be depressed adolescents and then depressed adults.

CASE HISTORY
A DEPRESSED, SITUATIONALLY
STRESSED CHILD

Michael is a kindergartener whose parents are separated. He lives with his mother and her boyfriend, Rich. There are frequent fights in the house and Rich, whom Michael adores, has left home several times, threatening never to come back. Following a particularly bad argument, Rich left the house and became involved in a motorcycle accident, which almost killed him. Michael was at the hospital with his mother and saw Rich immediately after the accident.

Following the accident, Michael's behavior in school became disruptive and very aggressive. He would literally explode in the classroom, throwing pencils and crayons, and tearing papers. After the outburst Michael would crawl under the table or hide in the closet. Michael then began to run away from school. The most recent time he ran away, he was found lying in a stream, wishing he were dead.

MASKED DEPRESSION

Advocates of the symptom perspective hypothesize that depression may not be expressed directly by children, but instead is "masked" and expressed behaviorally by various symptoms. Masked depression can be expressed in the classroom as boredom, restlessness, fatigue, problems with concentration and behavior, and complaints of illness. Indeed, from this perspective, many of the so-called "acting-out" behaviors or conduct disorders are signs of depression.

Glaser (1968) suggested that even though a child or adolescent does not present the typical picture of depression, that is of sadness and anhedonia (i.e., the inability to experience pleasure), there are elements of depression that are an integral part of a youth's functioning.

CASE HISTORY
A MASKED DEPRESSION

Thirteen-year-old Carol is repeating seventh grade, at her parent's insistence. Her parents also requested a psycho-educational evaluation for Carol. Their major concern was her failing grades. The school's concern was the behavioral difficulties that they were experiencing with Carol.

For the past two years, Carol has received failing grades in all subjects, and her behavior has also deteriorated. There have been numerous in- and out-of-school suspensions.

Carol exhibits a variety of behaviors in the classroom that are all aimed at being the center of attention. These behaviors range from talking aloud, making mouth noises, talking back or being a "smart-mouth" to teachers, and disrupting the class by dropping books or making other loud noises. Outside the school, Carol has been involved in shoplifting and sexual activities. At home, Carol is either in her room with the stereo on at full volume, or on the phone. Her mother is concerned that Carol does not eat, but her father believes Carol is not hungry because of all the junk food she eats during the day. Except for setting the table, Carol has no chores or responsibilities. She does not receive an allowance.

During the first therapy session, Carol was unable to keep up the facade of "everything's OK." She spoke of a previous suicide attempt where she had tried to cut her wrists but was stopped by her best friend. She felt that she had no future, that no one cared about her, and that life itself was too hard. Carol felt that she was ugly on the outside just as she was on the inside, and that she was fat. In reality, Carol is a very beautiful girl.

MASKED DEPRESSION
OR LEARNING DISABILITY?

Some masked-depressive children, after relatively good academic functioning, will develop symptoms that are similar to those with a specific learning disorder or an attention deficit disorder. Symptoms are similar as there is a loss of concentration and attention, and there may be hyperactivity, distractibility, and poor academic performance. A key indicator is the age and grade level at which a diagnosis is made. If records indicate average to good academic performance, this may suggest depression rather than any type of learning disorder.

CASE HISTORY
A CHILD WITH SYMPTOMS OF A
LEARNING DISABILITY

Danny is an eleven-year-old, sixth grade student who was referred to the school psychologist for academic difficulties. He was described by his teacher as having a short attention span, being highly distractible, and unable to follow directions. Academic work in all areas was extremely poor. Reading and spelling seemed to be especially difficult for Danny. Peer difficulties were also noted.

Individual achievement testing indicated that Danny was below grade level, approximately one standard deviation below expectation, whereas his intelligence testing displayed a large descrepancy between his low-average performance and superior verbal IQs. A classroom observation confirmed the teacher's comments of Danny's high distractibility and short attention span. Due to the school system's criteria for psychoeducational testing and a large backlog of referrals, there was no other testing or information collected. Based on this information, Danny was placed in a learning disability resource room for one period a day.

Danny's behavior continued to deteriorate and soon he was at the principal's office more than he was in the classroom because his disruptive behavior began to affect the other students. The culmination of events occurred when Danny had a fight with the vice-principal and ran away from school. He was missing overnight.

Family contact was made by the school social worker. It was during this "informal" interview that Danny's father revealed that Danny's mother had left the house several months before and was living in another town with her boyfriend and "new son." Danny was deeply upset that he had been "replaced," yet he felt a loyalty to his mother and could not talk of the desertion.

Reviewing Danny's prior academic achievements revealed that he had always been a B–C student. Group achievement tests also revealed that he was within grade level. Although on the surface Danny may have appeared to have a specific learning disability, depression was the real problem. Personality testing, information concerning prior behavior and achievement, and a parental interview could have resulted in the appropriate placement.

DEVELOPMENTAL PERSPECTIVES

As previously mentioned, the DSM III (American Psychiatric Association, 1980) assumes that the essential features of a major depressive episode are similar in infants, children, adolescents, and adults, but that there are differences in the associated features.

Infancy depression is recognized by the child's sad appearance, immobility, and loss of appetite. There is frequent and seemingly inconsolable crying.

Although infancy depression is more clearly recognized by facial expression and behaviors, recognizing depression in children is much more difficult due to the variety of symptoms presented. Some children may present a picture of an active conduct disorder, whereas others may be seen as quiet, compliant, and withdrawn or shy. What seems to be common features of depression in both the "acting-out" and the "compliant" children are mood disturbance and anhedonia. In addition, many depressed children feel that they can't do anything right and exhibit excessive self-criticism.

In adolescents, negativistic or frankly anti-social behaviors may appear. Feelings of wanting to leave home or of not being understood and approved of, restlessness, grouchiness, and aggression are common. Sulkiness, a reluctance to cooperate in family ventures, and withdrawal from social activities (with retreat to one's room) are frequent. School difficulties are likely. There may be inattention to personal appearance and increased emotionality, with particular sensitivity to rejection in love relationships. Substance abuse may develop.

STRESS IN DEPRESSION

Depression is usually a reaction to a combination of many stress factors. One isolated stress does not mean that the child or adolescent will become depressed. However, if the child or adolescent is experiencing several stresses over a short period of time, stresses such as a significant loss, family and/or personal conflicts, or physical or mental parental illness, then there could be a high risk for depression.

Confusion and conflict within the family due to social and economic disturbances can disrupt familiar boundaries and guidelines. Adolescents, as well as children, are at a loss of what to expect, along with a feeling of no support.

Adolescents are concerned with their bodily image and have an idealized version of what they wish to look like. Typically, adolescents are aware of and concerned about the least bit of physical change such as pimples, weight and/or height, or breast or genital size.

LOSS IN DEPRESSION

For children and adolescents, the stress that can occur through loss is not only the obvious loss of a significant person through death, divorce, separation, or family relocation, but also for a loss of childhood, loss for the familiar boundaries and guidelines, loss of an ideal body image, loss of self-esteem, or loss of goals.

The loss of childhood presents to adolescents physical, social, and emotional changes. Changes that are indicative of growth can also be frightening to some individuals. New alliances are formed that are outside of the family. With the forming of new friends, there is also the questioning of family standards and values. Adolescents feel the need to establish independence and relinquish their dependence on parents. With increased independence comes increased responsibility and, for some adolescents, there may be some very confused feelings of ambivalence. They feel a need to fit in with their peers and find acceptance, along with balancing the stresses put on them by parents, school, and society in general.

For both adolescents and children, a physical illness can cause a great deal of stress, especially if the illness sets them apart from their peers.

A loss of self-worth and self-esteem can be triggered by feelings of parental and/or peer rejection when expectations are not met. Just as adolescents are acutely conscious of the least bit of physical change, they are also acutely aware of and tend to exaggerate their shortcomings. They often feel limited in what they are able to accomplish and are overly sensitive to real or imagined criticism or rejection. Oftentimes parents will reject a trait or fault in their child or teenager that they feel within themselves. A woman may reject her daughter's femininity, perhaps because she is threatened or frightened by her own femininity. Parents may reject their child's ambitions because of their own felt inadequacies. To have a doctor in the family is more important to those parents than the child's own desire to be a teacher. Parents who do not listen to their child give the message that he or she is not worth listening to. And thus, another blow to self-worth and self-esteem occurs.

Loss of goals can occur any time, even when things are going well. This loss is hard to understand. When an adolescent wins or achieves a goal there should be a sense of accomplishment. Instead, for some, there is a feeling of "So what?" accompanied by a sense of loss. Examples of letdowns are making the honor role, finishing high school, or winning a dirt bike race. Sometimes victories are too stressful for the vulnerable youth.

PHYSICAL MANIFESTATION
IN DEPRESSION

There is general agreement that depression can manifest itself not only psychologically and behaviorally, but physically as well. Our inherently strong mind-body correlation exemplifies how emotional upsets can trigger an assortment of illnesses. These illnesses are very real and should not be dismissed lightly. Belittling or labeling a child or adolescent as a "baby" or a "hypochondriac" does not take away the pain.

Although many instances of depression can be due to environmental or psychological stress, biological research into a predisposition or a biological weakness to depression in children and adolescents has only just begun. Manic depressive episodes have been thought to be rare in prepubertal children. However, as research expands and diagnostic criteria become clearer, perhaps a biological connection can be made.

RESEARCH IN DEPRESSION

The dearth of research on children's depression has resulted in more questions than answers regarding the developmental progressions and changes in the expression of depressive feelings. What has been realized is that there are children who are sad and in need of support.

Rosenthal and Rosenthal (1984) worked with sixteen suicidal preschoolers, from ages 2½ to 5 years. In comparing behaviorally disordered preschoolers to suicidal preschoolers, these researchers found that the suicidal preschoolers had a higher rate of running away and nonsuicidal aggression directed toward themselves, and had more depressive symptoms and less pain and crying after injury. In addition, suicidal children were more likely to be victims of child abuse or neglect and were more likely not to be wanted by their parents. They exhibited more feelings of abandonment and despair. They had fantasies of family reunion and hopes of changing their painful life.

To assess the relationship between depression and suicidal behavior, Cohen-Sandler, Berman, and King (1982) compared suicidal children, depressed children, and children with other psychopathologies. Their study suggested that not all depressed children are suicidal, and that it is possible to distinguish between those children who are suicidal and those who are depressed but without suicidal ideations. Of the one hundred symptoms evaluated in the study, only two symptoms were felt to reflect significant differences between suicidal children or depressed children. Those children who were suicidal displayed both an internal and external aggression. The suicidal children exhibited a depressed affect which combined with an outward aggression toward individuals in their environment. When used with a developmental history, a diagnostic interview, and a review of the child's stresses within the immediate past, knowledge of these two symptoms enhances prediction.

In a research study of depressive symptoms and suicidal behavior in adolescents (Robbins and Alessi, 1985), it has been suggested that adolescents are reliable reporters of their own symptoms. The study indicates that an adolescent's expressed seriousness in his or her intent to die is highly associated with lethality of the behavior. The more intense the reported suicidal feelings are, the more dangerous the behavior is likely to be. The study also found that those who made previous nonlethal attempts are at higher risk for more serious attempts at some future time. Another important symptom for suicidal behavior is depressed mood. When alcohol or substance abuse becomes part of the clinical picture, then there is an increase in the risk of multiple attempts and lethality. Therefore, intense self-expressions of suicidal feelings, dangerous behavior, previous attempts, depressed mood, and alcohol and/or substance abuse are all highly significant symptoms.

Depression in children and adolescents *does* exist. Recent estimates state that from three to more than six million children and adolescents in the United States suffer from depression, most of which is unrecognized and untreated. Without intervention, how many will grow up to be depressed adults or end in suicide? Although all children and adolescents who are depressed do not kill themselves, depression is still a major factor in suicide.

CHAPTER 3

Family Patterns

Many investigators believe that suicidal behaviors in children and adolescents are symptoms of underlying family disruption, as well as the youth's own distress (Morrison and Collier, 1969; Pfeffer, 1981a; Sabbath, 1969; Bender and Schilder, 1937). Family patterns that appear to be significantly related to a youth's suicidal behavior include the loss of a significant parenting figure before age twelve, genetic predisposition, communication barriers between parent and child, and ineffectual parenting skills (Lourie, 1967; Pfeffer, 1981a; Stanley and Barter, 1970).

LOSS

The loss of a parent figure before age twelve has a significant impact upon a child's susceptibility to suicide (Stanley and Barter, 1970). It is important to note that a parental death is more often a factor for those children who have completed a suicide than those suicide attempters who have experienced a parental loss through desertion or divorce (Dorpat, Jackson, and Ripley, 1965). Whether from death, separation, or divorce, family disruption appears to create a sense of isolation within children. Suicidal youths feel as if they have no control over their environment.

Loss of a parent removes or displaces the role model for many developing young people, which is a major factor in behavior patterns (Finch and Poznanski, 1971; McAnarney, 1979). Shaw and Schelkin (1965) note that the loss of a parent may result in the conditioning of a suggestible child, may precipitate anxiety and depression, may decrease the child's sense of self-worth, and may disrupt interpersonal relationships with others.

An equally dramatic impact on a child is the psychological loss of a parent. The psychological loss may stem from marital discord, violence, substance abuse, or medical and/or psychiatric illness. In the suicide attempters' families there is a higher rate of medical and/or psychiatric illnesses, in particular substance abuse and a history of suicide (Garfinkel, Froese, and Hood, 1982).

The ability of the youth to adjust to the loss of a parent is dependent on the nature of the loss, whether through death, divorce, or desertion; the developmental stage of the youth when the loss occurs; the youth's ego strength; the degree to which the youth has achieved independence; and the amount of support available and remaining in the family (Glaser, 1978; Ray and Johnson, 1983).

A study of thirty-four suicidal children (Morrison and Collier, 1969) found that 76% of the youths who attempted suicide experienced a significant loss, a separation, or the anniversary of a loss within days or weeks prior to their suicide attempts.

CASE HISTORY
PSYCHOLOGICAL LOSS
OF A FATHER

Allan, age seventeen, was failing all his subjects in school, was often truant, and lied frequently to his mother—not only about going to school but as to where he was during the day and/or evening and with whom he was associating. He was frequently in fights and was drinking and using drugs. He had a part-time job that he often neglected.

Following Allan's threat of suicide, the family sought counseling. At the first meeting, Allan's father stated he would not attend any further sessions since it was his son's problem. Subsequent meetings with Allan and his mother revealed a long history of neglect by his father. The father pursued his own interests and recreation and refused to talk to Allan whenever Allan got into trouble or disregarded the rules. His "silent treatment" simply angered Allan all the more and encouraged more negative acting out behaviors. This psychological loss of his father raised Allan's stress level to a point where suicide seemed to be the only means of dealing with his father's rejection.

GENETIC PREDISPOSITION

Although it is thought by some that suicide is neither inherited nor "runs in families," a history of suicide in a family is a significant risk factor for suicide. Blumenthal and Hirschfeld (1984) explain that the risk is possibly caused by identifying with the family member who committed suicide, genetic factors for suicide, and genetic transmission of psychiatric disorders. The authors state that studies have suggested a high agreement rate in suicides of identical twins, and that biological relatives have a greater increase in suicide than adoptive relatives. They also cite a study of the Amish, who have a 300-year history of basic isolation within its own group, which revealed twenty-six suicides over the period from 1880 to 1980. All but two of the suicides could have had a diagnosis of affective disorder, a disturbance of mood, accompanied by a full or partial manic or depressive syndrome. Blumenthal and Herschfeld feel the research suggests a possible genetic factor in both suicide and in affective disorders.

Research by Pfeffer, Conte, Plutchik, and Jerrett (1979) support the finding that parents of suicidal childen are often depressed and suicidal. These children appear to identify with their parents' depression and to feel hopeless and helpless in altering their environment. While not discounting a genetic predisposition for an affective disorder and/or suicidal modeling by parents or close friends, the fact remains that there is an increased risk of suicidal behaviors for these children.

Some children and adolescents who have a biological predisposition to an affective illness experience added stress in coping with any crisis. Although manic-depressive illness, which is an affective disorder, has been thought to be rare in young children, some young children do experience endogenous depression or biochemical depression. Children and adolescents with a biological predisposition to depression may be at high risk for suicide when dealing with psychological and social stress (Gilead and Mulaik, 1983).

Explanations for the increasing risk of suicide in children and adolescents who come from a family with a history of suicide include not only identification with the suicide but also with the genetic tendency toward psychiatric disorders. Blumenthal and Hirschfeld (1984) also report a study of psychiatric inpatients which revealed that half of those individuals with a family history of suicide had made a suicide attempt, and that over half the parents in a family with a history of suicide had a diagnosis of an affective disorder. The authors also report that twenty-four of twenty-six suicides among the Amish could have been diagnosed as major affective disorders, which suggests that possible genetic factors exist not only in affective disorders but in suicide as well.

CASE HISTORY
GENETIC PREDISPOSITION

Matthew was adopted when he was three years of age. His mother, who had severe bouts of depression, had provided only minimal care of Matthew since birth. Most of his care was provided by various foster mothers. Upon placement into a supportive and loving home, the child began to thrive.

When Matthew was eight years old his adoptive parents became concerned about his "blue moods." There appeared to be no reason for Matthew's depression and Matthew himself could report only that he "woke up feeling sad." During his down periods, Matthew was withdrawn, cried periodically without apparent cause, and was irritable.

Matthew continued to have periods of depression but it was not until he was fourteen years old that his behavior became more out of control. Matthew's moods became more pronounced and his school work dropped dramatically. Behavior was erratic, with temper outbursts occurring.

Matthew was hospitalized, with a diagnosis of Major Depressive Disorder, Recurrent.

COMMUNICATION BARRIERS

Pathological communication between parent and child creates a stress that could place the child at a high risk for suicidal behaviors. The ways that communication can be blocked or never even established are varied.

There are patterns of communication, both verbal and nonverbal, established in suicidal families that actually encourage a person to commit suicide. A person might ignore or not listen to someone who is trying to express his or her suicidal thoughts. It is not unusual for someone to turn and walk away upon hearing the first hint of suicidal talk. Sometimes a family member will cut off a person in the middle of a conversation if that conversation begins to focus on suicide. Verbally given messages that encourage a person to take his or her own life are also not uncommon. A child's efforts to express feelings of unhappiness, frustration, or failure are often unacceptable to parents. All of these patterns reinforce the feelings that children and adolescents have, which further isolates them. Often a suicide attempt is a way of breaking down the barriers to communication so that significant others will know how desperate the individual is (Peck, 1982).

For those children who have a physically ill parent, neither the parent nor the children will share problems, as both want to protect the other. Children of psychiatrically ill parents develop communication skills that protect them from negative parental interactions (Garfinkel, Froese, and Hood, 1982). Unfortunately, these communication skills are ineffectual and counterproductive to survival (Pfeffer, 1981b).

The "expendable child" concept is another form of a pathological communication pattern. Sabbath (1969) first postulated the hypothesis that certain parents have a conscious and/or unconscious belief that a child is bad or is a burden. When such attitudes are conveyed directly and/or indirectly to the child, the child activates a wish to die. (An example of this is seen from our own clinical experience. Richie was an unwanted five-year-old child. He had been told repeatedly by his mother that he was a "bother" and was the cause for his father's desertion. The mother stated that she "would be happy" if Richie was not around. In his kindergarten class, Richie began to fight with his peers and attempted to cut his arm with a pair of scissors. Frequent accidents occurred, with each accident becoming more serious until he finally succeeded in ending his life in a "bike accident.")

Communication can be a barrier instead of the bridge that it should be. If good communication habits are not fostered when children are young, then in the later adolescent years the barriers may serve to keep the adults at a distance. The following are examples of some of the more typical types of communication barriers (McCoy, 1982).

1. Generational Separation: This barrier to communication is used effectively by children, adolescents, and adults. The result of this barrier is that both generations believe that the other has nothing to offer them. There are usually very universal statements to begin the blocking process. For example:

"When I was your age, I didn't have life this easy. I had to get out of school and work. You—you've got your own TV, stereo, and car. What more could you want?"
"My parents don't know a thing about sex."
"What does she know? She's just a baby."
"My folks are so dumb."

Each side has an opinion but neither side is listening.

2. Put-downs or Labeling: Often adults believe that if they can "label" a behavior for a child or adolescent, then the individual can see it and then change his or her ways. Once the behavior is identified, many adults feel that they have "done their job." Unfortunately what occurs is that the adults have

managed to distance and deny any responsibility for the problem. The child is left with feelings of anger and a damaged self-esteem, with little motivation for change.

"Why are you always so stupid?"

"My child wouldn't be that dumb. I must have got the wrong kid at the hospital."

"You're nothing but a bum and a troublemaker."

"If you weren't such a brat your father never would have left."

"You're a jerk."

"What are you? Some sort of clown?"

"You've been a troublemaker ever since you've been in this school."

Being constantly ignored and/or put down not only establishes the feeling of low self-esteem but effectively stops the youth from attempting any communication.

In some instances the child or adolescent, if put down or labeled in front of his or her peers, will try to live up to the reputation.

3. Power Plays: In a power play, each side has its own motivations and goals that are usually exclusive from the other side. The power play cycle is often composed of verbal habits. McCoy (1982) describes these habits as verbal ordering, prescribing, and lecturing. Examples of ordering are:

"Don't sit around the house moping all day. Get out and do something."

"Because I want you to do it."

"Stop the hysterics. I don't want to hear it."

"You could do it if you really wanted to."

Examples of prescribing are:

"Your problem is that you're lazy and don't apply yourself."

"If you would only. . . . "

"I told you that you'd make a mess if you did it that way."

"Here, let me do it."

Examples of lecturing are:

"If you had listened to me in the first place, you wouldn't be in this mess."

"There are other fish in the sea."

"Rome wasn't built in a day."

The youth's response to these verbal habits may range from the closed-ear and the tune-them-out rebuttal, to tactical agreement ("O.K. I'll do it in a minute") to angry acting out (such as slamming things around or storming out of the classroom).

These verbal habits convey to the child or adolescent that he or she has no control and that the adults are not at all interested in what the child or adolescent's feelings are. The breakdown in communication is then complete as neither side is listening to the other. What emerges are angry feelings and issues that are now harder to resolve.

4. Social Front: Some parents are thoroughly caught up in their status within the community. They see their children as not conforming to their standards of behavior or achievement. These parents may nag, ridicule, or withhold favors—all to no avail. Their children do not listen and seem to go out of their way to "embarrass" them. Often these children feel as if they are only objects. Some of these parents feel as if they should have total control over their children. A common theme with this type of parents is that their children should accept the parents' ideas, goals, and values. The children see their parents as being only concerned with what others think about them. These children feel very much alone and are unable to share with their parents their own hopes, goals, and dreams. If the child tries to establish his or her autonomy, the parent views the child as rebellious and ungrateful, whereas the child views the parent as unapproachable and tyrannical.

"What will the neighbors think if you don't go to college? I want you to go to Yale."

"What do you mean you want to go to art school? What

are you, some kind of fag or something? Just wait til the guys hear about you."

"B+ is nice but why didn't you get an A? The Smith's daughter made the honor roll."

"I don't want you to date Tom. His father is a drunk and he's going to be just like him."

In reverse situations, children have also become adept at the social front game.

"Mom, you are so out of date."
"Not fair."
"You are so fat you gross me out."
"You're from another spaceplane."

The message is clear: The receiver is lacking as a worthwhile person. Why else wouldn't the individual be accepted for the way he or she is?

5. Mixed Messages: Saying one thing and meaning another is a very common cause of communication confusion and blockage. This is an especially important issue to teenagers who are in the process of attempting to become independent and trying out a "new identity." If there are no clear-cut rules or standards for the youth to fall back on, the growing up process is harder.

A mixed message can sour a success, cause confusion, indicate that a parent is not really proud of the child, sabotage enjoyment, suggest that an achievement was not worthwhile, and place a youth in a no-win situation. Examples of mixed messages are:

"Yes, you can go cruising but I'll worry about you the whole time you're gone."

"I'll really be proud of you when you graduate from college."

"So, big deal, you made the second-string football team."

"How come, if you're so smart, you didn't make first honors?"

By giving mixed messages, the parent may actually be encouraging an undesirable behavior.

However, parents are not the only ones who give mixed messages. Often younsters will give behavioral, feeling, and/or verbal clues that indicate possible suicidal intent. For instance, they may withdraw from family and friends, show a decline in school performance, increase risk taking, run away, or act out in many ways. They may deny feelings and problems, become depressed or sad, cry excessively, and/or exhibit anger and hostility. They may even make direct statements, such as "I feel like killing myself," or indirect statements such as "I can't go on like this." Yet, when the youth is confronted with the possibility of suicide, there is a strong denial. He or she will often say, "I was joking," or "I didn't mean what I said," or "I was just having a bad day." It is difficult to deal with any youth who denies such feelings.

A recent example of such denial was the case of an eighth-grade boy who was despondent over failing grades. A classmate had alerted the police of his friend's suicide intentions. When the police and fire department emergency crew arrived at the boy's home, he assured them he was only joking. A search of the home failed to turn up any weapon, and the chief of police later described the boy as "calm, his attitude was good, and there was no indication of self-hysterics." Soon after the authorities left, the boy shot and killed himself with a 12-gauge shotgun (*New Haven Register,* 1987).

Denial is also used with mental health workers. It is not unusual for children and adolescents who have attempted suicide to deny their act, possibly out of fear of their own behaviors or fear that they will be thought to be mentally ill. Reaching these children is difficult, but not impossible, and it is important for the mental health professional not to give up. The use of active listening, working with the family, as well as working with the youth will often open up communication.

6. Over–Under Reacting: Although this communication barrier is not as serious as some of the others, the over–under reaction can still stymie communication.

An adult who overreacts can cause a child or adolescent such distress and/or guilt that he or she will hide a problem so as to not upset the adult. In an effort to show concern, an adult may ask too many questions. For some children and adolescents this may serve as nothing more than a turnoff. The questions, while meant to be full of concern, might be perceived as intrusive or even hostile. It is better to ask those questions that are important and to establish an open environment for communication. Oftentimes, asking questions will sidetrack a youth from what he or she really wants to talk about.

The underreacting adult minimizes what a child or adolescent feels is a major issue, feeling, or problem. Being told "It doesn't matter" or "Don't get so upset" only conveys to the child or adolescent that the adult does not understand and/or is not willing to share the feeling or the pain that the youth may be having. Underreacting adults may also withdraw from the youth by making little or no eye contact, by reading or doing some sort of work while the child or adolescent is talking to them, or by physically distancing themselves from the youth.

GOOD COMMUNICATION PATTERNS

Good communication patterns consist of both listening and talking. It is one thing to feel acceptance toward a child; it is quite another to have that child feel it. Gordon (1975) suggests that adults show acceptance nonverbally as well as verbally. Allowing a child to be active without intervention, as long as that activity is safe and acceptable, shows an acceptance and confidence in that child. Passive listening—saying nothing—conveys the fact that the child is worth listening to.

Gordon suggests simple "door-openers" or "invitations to say more." Some of these are:

"Tell me more about it."
"I'd like to hear about it."
"Let's discuss it."
"Tell me the whole story."

More successful than passive listening is active listening. Gordon explains that in active listening, the receiver tries to understand what the sender is feeling. The receiver then puts his or her understanding into his or her own words so that the sender can then react to it. This process allows misunderstandings to be cleared up before feelings are acted upon or repressed. An example of active listening follows:

Mother: "Would you please do the dishes?"
Daughter: "I always have to do the dishes!"
Mother: "You're angry at me because I asked you and not your sister."
Daughter: "Yes, she never does anything!"

Ideally, parents and educators should use a normal conversational tone when talking with children. Giving explanations or asking questions should be the same as when talking with friends. It is important for adults not to speak one way with children and another way with other adults. Asking open-ended questions, which need answers other than a response of "yes" or "no," is an excellent way to elicit communication (Good and Brophy, 1978).

INEFFECTIVE PARENTING SKILLS

Children who experience nonsupportive, unpredictable, or overtly hostile environments tend to develop characterological limitations. These characterological limitations prevent children from learning appropriate problem-solving techniques. Several studies point out that rigidity in thought processes is related to suicide (Levenson, 1984; Patsiokas, Clum, and Luscomb, 1979). These deficits in cognitive problem-solving abilities result in maladaptive and even self-destructive coping strategies in highly stressful situations. Suicidal children make cognitive errors in overestimating the seriousness of their problems and by not considering enough solutions to the problems. Going one step further, children with poor coping strategies are not able to utilize effectively the intervention and interaction strategies that may be offered to them. Garfinkel, Froese, and Hood (1982) found that 63% of suicidal youths had previous contact with psychosocial services. Psychological autopsies of successful suicides indicate that there had been professional contacts made months prior to the completed act. Obviously, these contacts were not enough to alter the felt stresses.

Pfeffer (1981a) has hypothesized a number of features of a suicidal child's family system. (We have seen these features, which contribute to ineffective parenting skills, in our treatment of suicidal children and adolescents.) She feels there are conflicts derived from unresolved childhood traumas when (1) parents are unable to separate from their families of origin, (2) the parent's family of origin strongly influences the choice of spouse and feelings toward a spouse, (3) parental feelings are projected onto the child instead of each other, (4) a suicidal child may have an especially close attachment to one parent, and (5) the family sees any change as a threat to the survival of the family.

Given these possible factors, and seeing that many suicidal children and adolescents are living with broken families due to separation and/or divorce, it is not difficult to accept the possibility of poor structure, discipline, and inconsistency in child-rearing practices as influences in suicide. Added to this may be parental problems with drugs, alcohol, mental illness, and, in many cases, some suicidal behavior.

Rigid Rearing Practices

Many parents have poor or ineffectual parenting skills. Some are extremely rigid and structured, thereby leaving little room for any independent action by the child. There is only one way to do things, and that is the parents' way. Any other way brands the youngster as rebellious, uncooperative, and a behavior problem. (We have seen in our own clinical experience one family in which the son, an adolescent, was exhibiting many negative behaviors, from smoking, drinking, and drug use to sexual promiscuity and threats of suicide. The parents stated that they didn't like him and could not openly say they love him. When asked to name some of their son's good qualities, they could name none!)

Unstructured Rearing Practices

To the other extreme, there are parents who establish little structure or discipline and give in to the child's every whim. They attempt to keep the child happy at all times and at all costs. Any exhibition of anger on the part of the child is met with guilt and threat by the parents. An example of one such family would be: Parents give in to all demands made by their daughter in fear that she would get angry. Every time she did get upset, the parents would attempt to soothe her by buying her toys and gifts.

Inconsistent Rearing Practices

A third type of rearing practice is demonstrated by parents who are split on their approach to their children. In one case the father is rigid and domineering and the mother is passive and dependent. Often the child identifies with the mother since the mother attempts to compensate for what she sees as unreasonable demands made by the father. Mother and child band together against the father. (A family we have recently seen has a mother who consistently attempts to make up for what she sees as unreasonable demands by the father. When the son's car was taken away due to his drunk and reckless driving, the mother either drove her son where he wanted to go or loaned him her car. When the son's allowance was cut off because he was employed part-time, the mother continued to give him money without the father's knowledge.)

FAMILY PATTERNS AND SUICIDE

Why some family patterns result in suicide or suicide attempts as opposed to developing other psychological disturbances is unclear. Peck (1982, p. 3) states that "youngsters grow up with little clear-cut guidance, confused or absent values, and a sense of floating along in time without direction." They may grow up without having any real hope for the future. Without hope, there is no reason to keep motivated, no reason to struggle, and no reason to continue to live.

Brown (1985) developed an approach to youth suicide based on Bowen's (1978) theory of "triangulation." The theory, based on psychopathology in families, points to the constant potential for imbalance in triads within families. The triad can become imbalanced and pathological, leaving one person hurt and/or omitted. The imbalance also allows a way for expressing or storing strong negative emotions. Within families, the triad may consist of father, mother, and child. It can also consist of father and mother together, a child, and that child's sibling.

Balancing the relationship in a triad is a continuous process and a way of validating the existence and acceptance of those within the triad. Any imbalance, such as parents favoring one sibling over the other, often effectively shuts the other sibling out of the validation process. Unless positively validated over the years, feelings of negative self-worth and a poor self-concept will most likely develop. Brown suggests that this loss of validation, the "loss of place," may be a prelude to self-destructive behaviors. There is a disruption in the development of one's sense of self and the ability to integrate emotions, particularly in adolescence. The depression, the "emotional aloneness," that could result may be serious enough to push that youngster to suicide. He or she may choose suicide over some other disturbance since there is a feeling of not existing in the eyes of significant others anyway.

CASE HISTORY
INEFFECTUAL PARENTING
SKILLS

Thirteen-year-old Lynn entered family counseling along with her parents and younger eight-year-old brother,

Roger. The parents had been having marital difficulties and were thinking of divorce. Family therapy was the last step.

As family therapy progressed, it quickly became obvious that the children had formed alliances. Lynn was allied with her father, and Roger with his mother. The children felt that they had to take a side. To add to the stress, each parent felt out of control and blamed the other for "turning our child against me." Lynn and Roger were depressed and felt that they were the cause of the family's difficulties. Although both children described their sibling as a "brat," they were very close to each other.

Each child constantly tested the limits of the parents. Demands were made and granted, expensive gifts were given, and no responsibilities were asked of the children. Feeling the family unit breaking apart, with no clear rules or structure, drove the children into a frenzy of acting-out behaviors. When Lynn's first boyfriend dumped her for her best friend, Lynn made a suicide attempt.

Each parent blamed the other and no one listened to Lynn. Roger, confused by the events, became increasingly aggressive and tried to get even for his sister by hiring some older kids to beat up the ex-boyfriend.

The parents' parenting techniques let the children have whatever they wanted and made no demands. After all, they were "just babies." Whenever there was an issue or a problem to be resolved, the parents openly disagreed with each other, which left the children to make their own choices.

SUMMARY

The family pattern dynamics suggest that children who are prone to suicide experience a high pattern of family disruption before the age of twelve, and that these disruptions could result in the establishment of pathological communication and ineffective problem-solving strategies. Family disruptions can occur by losing a parent through death, divorce, or separation; by disturbed psychological and emotional relationships; by aggressive and hostile parenting; and/or by physical and/or mental illness. When there is a culmination of stresses, these factors can lead to suicidal behaviors.

CHAPTER 4

Perceptions of Death

CHILDREN'S VIEWS AND ATTITUDES TOWARD DEATH

Young children who engage in suicidal behavior often have inaccurate concepts of death. Piaget (1923) theorized that at age six or seven years, a child believes that anything that is active is alive. At ages seven to eleven, there is a cognitive awareness of the finality of death, and a mature and cognitive interpretation of death occurs around the adolescent years.

In his studies with children ages three to ten years, Nagy (1959) found that up until age five, death is felt to be temporary. Between the ages of five to nine, death is personified, with an awareness that it is irreversible. At around the age of nine, death is viewed as occurring for everyone and it is understood to be inevitable.

Young children appear to have a tenuous sense of the reality of mortality. Death is often viewed as a sort of magical fantasy place. Often children feel that after death they will be able to hover invisibly over the scene. They believe that they will be able to observe the effects of their actions (Garfinkel and Golombek, 1974).

Pattison (1977) concluded that very young children have no intellectual notions of death. From ages three to six years, death is viewed as possible and real but as not being permanent. For children up to age six, self-identity revolves around significant others. After age six, and up to the adolescent years, anxiety about death is manifested through a fear of bodily disfigurement and/or a loss of physical abilities and capacities.

Otte and DeBlassie (1985) reported that experts in the field find that three- to five-year-old children have a limited or erroneous understanding of death. It is seen more as sleep. For them, death is being less alive. They feel that movement in a coffin is limited and that dead people will eat, breathe, and grow. This age group also thinks that dead people know what is happening on earth. From age five to nine, children tend to personify death. They see it as an angel or a dead person who still walks, but they feel it is still something they can avoid.

Whereas the concept of the finality of death is not fully developed in very young children, the fact remains that children are engaged in suicidal behaviors for a variety of reasons. These reasons include conscious and unconscious fantasies, wishes, and fears.

Suicide is often the end point of manipulation. The child is attempting to manipulate others in order to gain love and affection, or to punish others, or to change an impossible situation (Bender and Schilder, 1937). These manipulation attempts, usually against the parents, are the child's effort to take control of a situation where there are feelings of vulnerability and helplessness (Jacobs and Teicher, 1969). "You'll be sorry when I'm dead," reflects the child's magical thinking. It is the child's fantasy of being in control and/or punishing others. This threat points out the child's limited comprehension of death's finality. There is the implication that the child will survive or be around to observe the effect of his or her actions (Garfinkel and Golombek, 1974).

ADOLESCENTS' VIEWS AND
ATTITUDES TOWARD DEATH

Adolescents, as well as children, often see death glamorized by television, movies, books, and magazines. In many cases, adolescents romanticize death and the way it will affect loved ones as well as people in general.

Often adolescents think of death as a peaceful sleep that will make everything better. They picture death as a means of punishing someone or as a way of forcing some significant others to express their love for them. Strangely enough, they believe that somehow they will be around to benefit from the punishment their death has caused or the love that is shown. It is not unusual for adolescents to gain much satisfaction from fantasies about death. Some children and adolescents see suicide and death as a way of being reunited with a parent, grandparent, sibling, or girl/boyfriend who has died. They may also see it as a way of expressing the great love they have for someone who has died or rejected them. McIntire, Angle, and Struempler (1972) feel that only 20% of adolescents aged thirteen to sixteen accept death as a total cessation of life. If this is true, then it adds credence to the thoughts and ideas of some adolescents that they will be around to witness the results of their suicide.

It is not unusual for adolescents to become preoccupied with thoughts of death and dying. They may even enjoy a sense of power over death in that they feel they can control the time and place that it will happen. And by choosing, through suicide, when and where they will die, they will achieve a sense of immortality. Death is also seen as an escape from their feelings of helplessness and hopelessness, so much so that they will focus on it and ultimately pursue it (Klagsbrun, 1981).

Years ago, most deaths took place in the home where the dying person was surrounded by members of the family. Children and adolescents, as well as adults, were familiar with death and the experience helped them view death as a normal part of living. In more recent years, most people die in a hospital and the majority of children reach adulthood without experiencing a death in the family. Thus, many young people have never been present at someone's death, and it is that lack of experience that makes it difficult to talk openly about death (World Book Encyclopedia, 1981).

Most adolescents and children think of death as being a long way off. Most of their life is still ahead of them and, even though they understand the finality of death in concept, it is too distant for them to be concerned. They are caught up in the everyday business of school, family, and social matters, enjoying the pleasures of the present. The quality of their life is often more important than their longevity. They are attempting to rid themselves of dependency on their family and to orientate themselves toward the future. There is not time to focus on death, unless it happens to someone they can identify with, and even then it is seen only as a transient process. It is not unusual for adolescents to get caught up in the emotions of the death of a fellow student who dies in an automobile accident and then speed dangerously down the highway the day after the funeral. It is also not unusual for adolescents to continue using and abusing alcohol and drugs even if these substances were responsible for contributing to the death of an acquaintance or friend. They deny death through a feeling of immortality even though they are aware of the reality of death. They see death as something that happens to others. Their great concern with the present makes the future and past relatively unimportant. Everything that is of importance in life is either in the present or immediate future (Kastenbaum, 1959). Although adolescents have an awareness that death is a final process for all living things, they, like most others, repress that knowledge and go about living their lives. Generally, it takes many years after adolescence for the reality and acceptance of death to become part of one's concept of life. It is repressed for as long as possible, usually until life events make continued repression impossible (Barman, 1976).

Seeing the adolescents' concept of death in this manner, one can see that it would take unusual pressure and stress for an adolescent to place his or her focus on death in terms of the present. It would mean a disruption of a normal growth process. To have adolescents face their own mortality and fear of death, a process they have avoided doing and/or perhaps not encouraged to do by family and society, is the result of their inability to cope and deal with life stresses and problems.

DEATH AS A CHOICE

Children and adolescents will use death as an escape from an intolerable living situation. As mentioned previously in Chapter 3, the youngster who shows suicidal behavior has fewer inner resources (i.e., coping and communication strategies) to fall back on during stressful times (Garfinkel, Froese, and Hood, 1982; Levenson and Neuringer, 1971). In pre- and early adolescence especially, there is an intensity in all feelings such as anger, sadness, and helplessness. Children see death as "the only way out" because they have few life experiences combined with poor problem-solving techniques.

CASE HISTORY
DEATH AS A CHOICE

Timmy is a nine-year-old boy with an alcoholic mother who provides only sporadic care. His father disappeared from the family before Timmy's birth.

Blamed for events that had gone wrong in his mother's life, Timmy became the focus of his mother's anger. Physical abuse was a way of life for him. In an attempt to escape from his mother, Timmy began to stay out on the streets.

While on the streets, Timmy quickly became a target for street gangs. To Timmy, both his home and the street were dangerous places. The only life that Timmy had experienced was the beatings by his mother and the dangers of the street.

Timmy was admitted to the hospital's emergency room due to a drug overdose. When questioned, Timmy expressed the wish to die. The future, as Timmy perceived it, was bleak with no hope and no help.

DEATH AS RELATED TO LOSS

The misconceptions of death may translate into suicide as a result of losses of any nature. The loss does not necessarily have to be the loss of a parent; it could be that of a friend, a pet, or even an intangible loss such as status or self-esteem.

To a child who fears a loss of status or self-respect because a test was passed with a C instead of the usual A, the imagined loss is just as real as a death. A loss can occur when a child feels he or she has been let down by someone on whom the child has been depending (Crumley, 1982). Whatever the loss, what emerges are strong feelings of hopelessness, and death may be seen as the only solution.

CASE HISTORY
LOSS OF SELF-ESTEEM

Anna, a senior in high school, was an A student and was not allowed by her parents to be involved in any extracurricular activities. She was under constant pressure from her parents for high academic achievement. They insisted on grades no lower than an A − average. Homework took priority over all nonschool-related activities.

Anna was having difficulty in a geometry course and could not bring herself to ask for help since she felt that she should be able to handle it by herself. She failed the mid-term exam and consequently received a grade of C on her report card. Her parents insisted that she limit social activities and concentrate on pulling her grade up. She was made to feel that she had not applied herself, although in her eyes she had put in a great deal of effort. Added to this was a break-up with her boyfriend and a rejection from one of her selected colleges. Feeling a loss of status and self-respect, and seeing no relief from parental pressure, Anna attempted suicide.

Another type of loss, discussed in Chapter 3, is the sacrifice of the "expendable child." The expendable child uses suicide to stop being a burden to a parent (Sabbath, 1969). This is suicide for love. When love and needs are not met, interpersonal intimacy is not successfully developed.

When a child's hostile perception of a parent is internalized, feelings develop that say to the child that he or she is bad and not a good person. This aggression turned inward is depression. Pfeffer (1981a) has hypothesized that, to a child, suicidal behavior is a last-resort mechanism to remove or to punish the negative self-perceptions.

ROLE REVERSAL

Role reversal, where a parent's need for nurturance is projected onto the child, seems to be a common occurrence in children with suicidal behaviors (Pfeffer, 1981b). The parent demands that the suicidal child fulfill a role of providing gratification and protection to the parent. To maintain this pathological support is often too overwhelming for the child, who then reverts to suicidal behavior to remove these stressors.

Section Two

Section Two will aid school personnel in recognizing situational, behavioral, and feeling signals of depression and suicidal behavior. In addition, myths of suicide will be discussed as well as sources of student stress in school and in the classroom.

CHAPTER **5**

Myths and Misinformation about Suicide

One problem that arises when dealing with suicide is the misinformation that abounds and thereby hinders our perceptions and reactions to suicide. Myths and misinformation have surrounded suicide since early times. Providing correct information and removing the mystery of suicide is an important educational and intervention process. Providing education workshops on suicide to various audiences, whether it be for teachers, parents, or students, exploring and/or exposing the myths of suicide is an important aspect of the prevention program.

DISPELLING MYTHS

There are many commonly accepted myths and much misinformation concerning suicide. The following information is not intended to be complete but will address some of the more widely accepted myths among the general population. Hopefully, shedding light on myths such as these will result in more knowledge and acceptance of the seriousness of child and adolescent suicide.

Myth: People Who Talk about Suicide Don't Do It

This myth provides a "crutch" to some people, allowing them to pass off of any responsibility toward taking action for stopping a suicide. Admittedly, it is difficult to ascertain if an adolescent or child means to kill himself or herself when statements such as "I'll just kill myself if John doesn't call me tonight" or "I wish I were dead" are heard in hallways and classrooms. How does a person know if statements such as these are serious or not? It is usually impossible to know. That is why it is so important to ask. It is better to appear foolish by asking a "dumb" question than risk taking a chance. Signals are sent of people's intentions in the hopes that someone will hear them (Grollman, 1971). Suicide threats must be taken seriously. When words fail to convey a person's desperation, then there may be a movement toward suicidal action.

Consider Bobby, who kept telling his teacher that he wished he were dead. He made this statement a number of times but always with a laugh and a denial that he was serious. The laugh and the denial convinced the teacher that Bobby was not serious, and no referral was made. Bobby then did make an attempt on his life.

Any such statement warrants a referral to an appropriate professional. Remember: People who talk about suicide do kill themselves.

Myth: Suicidal People Are Fully Intent upon Dying

Psychological autopsies of successful suicides of children and adolescents indicate that a large majority had previously verbalized their wish to die or had threatened suicide (Shafii et al., 1985). These verbalizations are efforts to gain attention, to obtain the help or the intervention to keep a person from taking that last desperate step.

There is an ambivalence about dying in most, if not all,

children and adolescents. They want to live but living is too painful. Most suicides occur in the home and at a time when intervention might be possible. Frequently, there are calls for help immediately following a suicide attempt. This reaching for help is indicative of the ambivalence about dying. Individuals often weigh carefully the pros and cons of living before deciding on suicide, and even then they are unsure that suicide is the solution.

Myth: People Need Only to Look on the Bright Side of Life to Feel Better

This overly simplistic view conveys to a suicidal child or adolescent that no one actually knows how he or she really feels. Children and adolescents do not have the life experiences to realize that situations and feelings do change. Being told that "things will look better tomorrow" only causes a depressed youth to feel more isolated and alone with his or her feelings. No one understands the pain that is felt as no one listens to what has been said. There is hearing without listening.

For example, Jim, an adolescent, was depressed and had confided to his teacher that he had thought of suicide. The teacher responded by pointing out all of Jim's positive traits and the many things that he should be thankful for, commenting that "you're in a slump and things will get better." He also pointed out that Jim's senior year was coming up and then college, stressing that because of Jim's excellent sports record a scholarship was a possibility.

What this approach fails to consider is that Jim is thinking of the present, not of the future, and that next year and college are not foremost in his mind. Many children and adolescents are not future oriented; they want or can deal only with the present. To look on the bright side is often not possible since their problems and emotions are overwhelming. They simply are unable to see or think of the bright side. This approach may also increase a depression and add guilt since the implication is that the individual should not feel that way. Remember: A depressed and suicidal person may be able to intellectualize about the good things of life but not believe in them.

Myth: People Who Make Suicide Attempts Are Only Looking for Attention

Unfortunately, many adults believe that child and adolescent suicides are "accidents" and that the youths did not really mean to hurt themselves. It is thought that these individuals were just fooling around and merely wanted "attention." Everyone wants attention, but for those children and adolescents who feel ignored, hopeless, desperate, and isolated, suicide becomes a viable choice. If the only way that our children can get "attention" is to fool around with self-destructive behaviors, then it is not only deadly but sad.

In reality, a suicide attempt is an indication that all other avenues of receiving help have been tried and have failed. The person sees no other alternative but to commit suicide as a way of easing his or her intense pain. Our feeling is that pain tolerance is extremely low for children and adolescents, perhaps due to our many advances in medicine where physical pain is often quickly alleviated by medication. When children and adolescents find no medication to take away the emotional pain or when they find no one is willing or able to help them, then suicide may be an alternative. A successful suicide ends the pain, but the suicide that fails conveys the cry for help. This cry for help needs to be listened to and addressed.

Consider the diabetic teenage girl who found that she was pregnant and that her boyfriend wanted nothing to do with her. She took an overdose of insulin and was rushed to the emergency room, where she claimed to have taken double the insulin because she had "forgotten" her morning dosage and took it a second time. The staff at the emergency room felt that she was depressed and that the overdose was an attempt at suicide. She admitted this to the emergency room staff but denied it when her parents arrived. The parents believed that their daughter was simply upset because of the pregnancy and had wanted to get her boyfriend's attention. Against the advice and recommendations of the hospital, the parents did not seek further help.

Myth: When People Begin to Show Signs of Improvement, the Crisis Is Over

In this case, a person who is depressed appears to be improving, or behavior problems may lessen, or a person will be seen as beginning to deal with his or her drug/alcohol problem. In fact, many suicides occur within a few months of this improvement. The reason for the improvement may simply be that the suicidal person has now made a decision to complete the suicide. Great anxiety is felt in the decision-making process. Once the decision is made, regardless of what the decision is, the anxiety usually lessens. This may be comparable to what happens to a suicidal person when improvement is seen. Thus, the period of improvement is a most dangerous time since it may suggest that a decision to commit suicide has been made. Also, once a person feels less depressed, he or she has more energy to carry out a suicide plan, thus increasing the risk.

A concerned parent initiated an appointment to discuss her daughter who appeared to be depressed. At the first visit, the mother said that in the past few days things were much better and perhaps she overreacted. Her daughter was no longer as depressed and things were going smoother at home and at school. Since a crucial time for any person who may be suicidal is when the depression seems to be lifting, the daughter was interviewed and admitted she had decided to commit suicide.

Myth: Talking about Suicide Puts the Thought into People's Heads

Many people think that talking about suicide will increase the possibility of it. They fear that discussing the topic with a youth who had not previously thought about suicide would then insure that the youth will now consider it. If children and adolescents are giving clues, by their general behavior, that they are contemplating suicide, then it stands to reason that discussing the thought with them will not be implanting a new idea. It is quite likely that their behavior is aimed at initiating the involvement of some significant person. If that significant person fails to ask or discuss the youth's feelings, then it reinforces the feeling that no one really cares.

An example of this is Debbie. Increasingly withdawn and anxious, Debbie was confronted with this new behavior by a teacher. When asked if she was thinking of hurting herself, Debbie admitted she was but felt relieved that someone knew and was willing to talk with her.

Another example is Mike, who showed some of the same behavior as Debbie. When he was confronted, he was puzzled by the teacher's concern since he was simply experiencing increased stress due to school and his new part-time job. When asked about suicide, Mike stated that he felt too good about himself to do anything so stupid but he appreciated the teacher's concern.

Even though Mike was not suicidal, it was better for the teacher to trust her feelings and inquire than to find her unacted suspicions verified by an attempted suicide.

Myth: Children Don't Know Enough to Kill Themselves

Most adults believe that children do not know the means nor have the capacity to act on their impulses to kill themselves. Another belief is that since many youths do not understand the finality of death, any attempt on their own lives is not intentional nor aimed at completion. Recent evidence disproves all the above. In the Rosenthal and Rosenthal (1984) study of sixteen suicidal preschoolers, age 2½ to 5 years, three children had made one suicide attempt, and the other thirteen had made multiple attempts. Rosenthal and Rosenthal report that children will admit to suicidal intent if that is indeed the case, thus concluding that children *do* know enough to kill themselves. It is suggested that adults begin to question children concerning their "accidents." Many deaths that have been labeled "accidental" may actually have been suicides. (We have seen children in our private practice who have given evidence of thinking, planning, and implementing a suicide attempt.) All adults need to have the awareness to ask the pertinent questions.

To review a case previously mentioned in Chapter 3, Richie and his mother were referred by a school psychologist to a mental health clinic. Richie repeatedly told the counselor that he was going to ride his bike in front of a truck so he could kill himself and make his mother happy. Richie finally succeeded in taking his life in the manner he described, in spite of the feelings of his counselor that children don't know enough to kill themselves.

Myth: People Who Make a Suicide Attempt Are Mentally Ill

Children and adolescents who attempt suicide are often thought of as socially and/or emotionally maladjusted. Children, adolescents, and adults will often avoid seeking professional help if they feel that by doing so they will be thought of as having serious emotional problems. There are many reasons aside from being socially or emotionally disturbed why children will reach a level where suicide is contemplated. Only a small percentage of adults who attempt or complete suicide have serious pathological problems. There is no evidence to date that this is not equally true for children.

Dennis is a boy of high-school age whose parents are in the process of a divorce. He recently broke up with his girlfriend, lost his part-time job, did not make the varsity basketball team, and was failing some of his subjects. Although Dennis was usually seen as a happy-go-lucky kind of guy, the stresses he was under caused him to be depressed and to contemplate suicide since nothing was going right. It was the stresses—not a mental illness—that caused him to consider suicide.

Myth: When a Child Develops Any Serious Acting-Out Behavior or Emotional Problem, or Attempts Suicide, the Parents Are Responsible

It is not uncommon in therapy for parents to hold themselves responsible for their children's actions and to ask themselves where they went wrong. Nor is it uncommon that many people do hold parents responsible. This view adds to the parents' guilt and feelings of responsibility. As we have long known, parents are often the last to see any danger signs in behaviors that may cause pain and/or problems for their children. They often deny what they see or make excuses for the behavior out of their love for their children. We have yet to see parents who have deliberately set out to cause their children pain and problems. In reality, what parents do is to use their best judgment in deciding on what they feel is appropriate at the time. There is no fault if things do not turn out favorably since parents did what they thought best at the time.

In our work with the survivors of children who kill themselves, we often see parents who keep replaying the circumstances of their child's suicide and their responsibility for it. They blame themselves and hinder their healing process by overfocusing on details that may or may not have made a difference. At this stage, we must convince parents that they did their best.

Myth: Drug/Alcohol Use and/or Aggressive and Hostile Behaviors Are Oulets for Anger and thus Reduce the Possibility of Suicide

The fact is that many children and adolescents use drugs and/ or alcohol to ease their pain and to escape from dealing with reality. Since alcohol and many drugs are depressants, they make a depressed person even more depressed, thus increasing the risk of suicide. Hostile and aggressive behavior is a reflection of a youth's hurt and it is a way of demanding immediate attention. These behaviors are indicators of a child's or adolescent's inability to deal with the stresses in his or her life, not indicators of anger and frustration. Drug and/or alcohol abuse is also considered a form of slow or hidden suicide.

Scott was an angry, acting-out young man who alienated everyone around him. He disrupted classes, rebelled against family and school, and was in trouble with the law for the use of drugs and alcohol. Instead of this behavior satisfying his anger and frustrations, it made him all the more isolated since many of his peers wanted nothing to do with him. Not seeing his behavior as responsible for the alienation he suffered, he blamed others and became more involved with drugs and alcohol. Feeling unable to adjust to his environment, he felt the only solution was suicide.

Myth: Childhood and Adolescence Is a Carefree, Troublefree Time of Life, Filled with Only Minor Problems and Adjustments

Many times, adults fail to see the fears and anxieties faced by children and adolescents as they attempt to adjust to an increasingly complex and confusing world. Greater technology, more world violence, higher educational demands, increased availability and use of drugs and alcohol, greater threats of venereal disease, increased peer pressures, and the climbing divorce rate and family disruption are only a few of the factors affecting today's children and adolescents.

Not all children come from happy, intact families. For example, nine-year-old Sue lives with her mother and her mother's boyfriend. She seldom sees her father and her relationship with her mother is tenuous due to her mother's boyfriend and his abuse. Sue is often left alone, is not adequately clothed or fed, and her personal hygiene is poor. Picked on at school, with impossible demands made upon her by teachers to pay attention, she frequently soils herself. This causes her embarrassment and results in being teased by other students. She spends afternoons and evenings in a home that is neither clean nor happy. This is hardly a carefree time in the life of this child.

Myth: Once People Contemplate or Attempt Suicide, They Must Be Considered Suicidal for the Rest of Their Lives

The fact is that most people, children and adolescents included, think of suicide for only a limited amount of time. Once the crisis has passed and the reasons for contemplating suicide are resolved, then suicidal ideation usually ceases. Although this may generally be true, we hold the theory that once suicide becomes a strong option for dealing with one's problems, then it will remain an option but one of much less priority. Future problems will be dealt with through a number of strategies but when all strategies fail, suicide may again be an option.

We theorize that people build a hierarchy of adjustment strategies and will choose their strategy for adjusting to a situation in some order. When they contemplated suicide, suicide was then a high priority in their hierarchy of adjustment strategies. Once they have resolved the issues that caused the suicidal thought or attempt and put into its place more appropriate adjustment strategies, then suicide as a means of dealing with situations is moved to a much lower position in the hierarchy.

Over time, myths become confused with reality. It is much easier to accept half-truths and to push away the painful uneasiness of suicide by believing in myths. To aid in stopping the suicide cycle among our young, these myths must be exposed.

Myth	**Fact**
People who talk about suicide don't do it.	People who talk about suicide *do* kill themselves. Talk of suicide, not wanting to go on anymore, despair, and hopelessness are cries for help. These are signals that need to be taken seriously.
Suicidal people are fully intent upon dying.	There is an ambivalence about dying. There is a need to end the pain but there is always the wish that something or someone will remove the pain so that life can continue.
People need only to look on the bright side of life to feel better.	For those who are thinking of suicide, it is difficult, if not impossible, to see the bright side of life. To acknowledge that there is a bright side only confirms and conveys the message that they have failed, otherwise they too could have a bright side of life.
People who make suicide attempts are only looking for attention.	It is true that people are looking for some attention, but they are looking for a way to ease their pain, for someone to hear their cries for help.
When people begin to show signs of	When a person's mood or behavior improves, it may

Myth	Fact
improvement, the suicide crisis is over.	be because the indecision concerning suicide is over. Finally making the decision eliminates the anxiety. That decision could be *for* suicide.
Talking about suicide puts the thought into people's heads.	If the clues are being broadcasted, talking about suicide won't put the thought there. It is there already. Talking about suicide removes the fears that the person is crazy and alone, and also takes away the guilt for thinking that way.
Children don't know enough to kill themselves.	Children *do* know how to hurt and/or kill themselves. Television provides the model, means, and methods. Significant others in a child's life may also provide the model of suicide as a way of solving a problem.
People who make a suicide attempt are mentally ill.	People who make a suicide attempt are stressed beyond their coping abilities. They aren't necessarily mentally ill. Depressed, yes. Stressed, yes. Mentally ill, rarely.

Myth	**Fact**
Parents are responsible if their child attempts suicide.	Parents do the best they can with the information and coping skills they have. There is often denial and disbelief because the thought is too frightening. Also, there are some parents who are too fragile emotionally and psychologically to meet the needs of their child.
Acting-out behaviors and/or substance abuse are outlets for anger and thus reduce the risk of suicide.	These behaviors are signals of poor adjustment and they reflect the frustrations these people feel. When the drug/alcohol use and/or acting-out behaviors are unsuccessful in dealing with their hurt and problems, suicide becomes a greater possibility.
Childhood and adolescence is a carefree, troublefree time of life, filled with only minor problems and adjustments.	Children are no longer as protected from outside influences as they once were. They are exposed to the harsh realities of the world at ages when they are most impressionable, thus contributing to their fears and anxieties.
Once people contemplate or attempt suicide, they must be considered	This is false in many cases. When the crisis is over and the problems leading

Myth	**Fact**
suicidal for the rest of their lives.	to suicidal thought are resolved, then suicidal ideation usually ceases. It is possible, however, for suicide to still be a subdued option for an individual, but as long as coping skills are adequate, it is not acted upon. When coping skills fail, then suicide may again become a strong option.

CHAPTER 6

Stress in the Schools

Many children get depressed but not all need to have professional intervention. How, then, does one determine when a child's sadness is something to be concerned about? Besides biochemical and neurotic factors, stress can also be a cause of depression. In understanding depression and how to prevent it before suicidal behaviors occur, one needs to look at the interactions and stresses of the child.

Stress is defined as the result of the frustration, conflict, and/or pressure a child or adolescent feels. Although stress does not always cause depression or lead to suicide, it is a major component to depression. Not everyone who is depressed commits suicide, but many who do commit suicide are depressed.

Teachers and others who are in the educational setting have great insight into children's behaviors but are often afraid to trust their own judgments. Teachers are not only able to observe a child in a particular setting but they are also able to compare that child with his or her peers. One of the prime responsibilities of a teacher is to be alert to and aware of possible implications of children's behavior in the classroom.

Our experience in the schools and with school-age children has led us long to be concerned with the causes of stress in the classroom and in the school in general. We recognize that teaching is a stressful profession. The majority of teachers are very nurturing and supportive and are able to help students who may be in crisis or under stress. These teachers, by their very caring, add to their own personal stress. Teachers should look carefully at their interactions with students so as to find ways to alleviate not only their stress but that of the children.

Although stress in and of itself may not be bad, and at times we all experience a high degree of stress, continued pressure placed on children from many sources could result in the breakdown of mental health, leading to depression and suicide.

Stress reactions involve the ego, that is, the way a person sees his or her own personality or self. To protect the self, a person builds up a number of defenses as a way of dealing with stress. Children and adolescents react in the same manner, using some type of defense or reaction to lessen the stress and to keep the self free from threat. Many of the behaviors seen in children in school are reactions to real or perceived threats.

Keep in mind that it is usually easier to prevent problems than to solve them. Students will "read" a teacher, regardless of any attempt the teacher makes to cover true feelings.

The way in which children and adolescents cope with stress is largely determined by their anxiety. Their anxiety reaction is formed by two perceptions (McNamee and McNamee, 1981):

1. Did the child or teen have any control or power to reduce, avoid, or terminate an event or situation, either real or imagined, that was stressful?
2. After the stressful event, were the resulting feelings positive in that the youth was able to "handle" the stress or was the youth left with feelings of vulnerability and helplessness?

When children and teens are unable to cope effectively with continuous stresses, depression and, for some of the more vulnerable children, suicidal behaviors result.

The complexity of the school and classrooms are too great to be able simply to identify stress and remove it. But if teachers and administrators become aware of how they contribute to the stress of children, then perhaps ways can be found to change their actions and behaviors to reduce that stress and yet remain effective educators.

STRESS AND TEACHERS

Attitude

A teacher's attitude toward children and his or her role as a teacher is a prime source of stress for children. It is difficult to like every individual child, but teachers must have an attitude of caring and respect for them in general. A child quickly senses whether a teacher likes or dislikes him or her and will often develop similar feelings for the teacher. If a child does not like the teacher, he or she often will not work for the teacher. The lack of success the student feels and the resulting pressure from the teacher to perform, along with the rejection the child feels, begins a cycle of stress.

Reducing stress Teachers often form opinions and make judgments about children and adolescents based on their behavior, what other teachers have said, or the youth's accummulative records. A simple and productive way of forming more positive opinions of children and adolescents is to spend a little time with each student individually to talk about the student and his or her likes, dislikes, dreams, aspirations, and expectations. One day spent in this manner will pay dividends for the school year.

Personality

By nature, some teachers are reserved, distant, and aloof. Children often find these teachers frightening and unapproachable but they will attempt to please the teacher through their work and behavior. However, when the teacher does not respond with warmth and friendliness, the children may feel they are responsible to some degree for the teacher's aloofness, thus making them uncomfortable. Continued behaviors such as these increase the children's stress since it seems no matter how hard they try or what they do, the teacher does not respond in a positive way. The children have no way of knowing that the teacher is this way because of his or her own growth and development, not because their behavior is poor.

Reducing stress Teachers do not have to be overly affectionate or warm. What they must convey to children is that they can be approached and that they will listen to and respect the students' thoughts and feelings. Meeting with students individually is a good way for teachers to communicate their feelings and expectations and to form a positive bond with the students.

Mannerisms

There are teachers who scream, use sarcasm, and speak in loud, harsh tones. They generally frighten children who often have little recourse but to accept it. Children may respond by developing behavior problems or by withdrawing. In most situations where there is confrontation by the teacher, he or she is generally the loser. In high school, for example, one teacher, who was a "screamer," challenged a student about his talking in class and insulted him by making unkind remarks. His response was to insult the teacher in return and walk out of the classroom. He had the last word and the teacher was humiliated in the eyes of the students.

Reducing stress There is no place for sarcasm in the classroom or school. Many teachers do not recognize that they speak in loud, harsh tones or even that they scream. Ask the opinion of a fellow teacher who has a classroom nearby. Ask other teachers for feedback that they hear from peers and students. Focus on talking in softer tones. When you feel your anger and frustrations rising, take a few minutes to step out of the room or change the subject. Try thinking and reacting to "I" feelings instead of "You" feelings. In other words, talk about how you feel about certain remarks or behaviors instead of focusing on the child and his or her remarks or behaviors.

Control

Some teachers attempt to overcontrol their students, whereas others have little control at all. Overcontrol keeps everyone, teacher included, on edge. The students must be careful not to overstep boundaries and the teacher must be on continual alert for those students who get out of line. Stress is a constant factor since the students can seldom relax while in the classroom.

Teachers who have little or no control add to children's stress because the students have few, if any, guidelines to follow in their behavior. Children need the security of knowing an adult is in charge and is able to bring order to the classroom. The uncertainty of not knowing how to react and respond adds to children's insecurity and raises their stress level. Some allowance must be made for the full spectrum of children's emotions. They should be allowed to be occasionally angry, bored, upset, tired, and unmotivated.

Reducing stress   Teachers must establish rules that are realistic for the age group in the classroom, not rules that are set to keep the teacher happy. A certain amount of noise, talking, and activity is healthy and can exist without being disruptive. As long as children operate within the framework of the rules, there is no reason to react. This narrows the amount of teacher reaction to serious violations of the rules. Rules must be set and the limits set by the rules are determined by the teacher's tolerance and good classroom management.

Mental Health

Some teachers, in reacting to and dealing with serious problems of their own, are in poor mental health. Some of the characteristics we have already discussed may be a reflection of poor adjustment. Many children feel the effects of a teacher's personal problems in the classroom. The more serious the problem, the more it may influence the students and the more it may create stress.

Children, while attempting to deal with their education, their own personal growth and problems, family adjustment and problems, and peer pressures, hardly need a teacher's problems also. Until the increasing severity of a teacher's problems becomes noticeable by other teachers or school administrators, children are subjected to the stress that teacher's behavior may cause. Obviously, teachers who reflect poor mental health through poor and ineffective classroom management should be encouraged to seek professional help to relieve their anxiety and stress. Teachers with serious adjustment problems should be relieved of their teaching responsibility.

Reducing stress Teachers who are in poor mental health may not recognize it. If they do recognize it, they may attempt to compensate for it by diverting attention to the behavior of others. It is the responsibility of all teachers to attempt to communicate to teachers with emotional problems that psychological help is available. If a troubled teacher is resistant to professional help and his or her students and classrooms are being affected, then the administration should be alerted. In serious cases, the teacher should be relieved of responsibilities until he or she is able to assume them again.

STRESS IN THE CLASSROOM

Testing

Although testing is a key factor in the measurement of learning, test construction is seldom taught in teacher education programs. Consequently, many tests constructed by teachers are neither valid nor reliable. Such tests often emphasize factual material that requires only memorization, thus students who are poor at memorizing are penalized. Often the tests are based on such a large segment of supposedly learned material that it is almost impossible to study for the test. Also, what the teacher feels is important may not be what the student sees as important.

The stress of studying for a test is further magnified when there is more than one exam to study for. Teachers often do not coordinate testing periods, hence two or more major tests may be given on the same day. This is often a reality at the high school level during final exams. It is not unusual for students to have two exams on one day and none on the next day. When this is done and when teachers place a high value on the test score in determining grades, the stress factor may be extremely high. Students learn early that tests are threats and they react to tests with great anxiety. Under the anxiety and stress, many perform poorly, again adding to their stress.

Reducing stress Too often, students are made to fit a schedule instead of the schedule being made to fit the students. There is absolutely no valid reason why tests and test periods cannot be coordinated between teachers and subjects. The stress of studying for more than one exam is great, given the emphasis most teachers place on tests.

There would also seem to be no good reason why a teacher cannot limit the focus of an exam or clarify important issues to be studied. Not only would this increase the success students will have on exams, but it ensures exposure to relevant material while making studying more manageable.

Unfamiliar test formats raise students' anxieties. A way to reduce this type of test anxiety is to review with the students a particular test's format. Keep in mind that stress is higher for verbal tests than for nonverbal tests.

It is also helpful to students to explain the purpose of a test. Make it clear that the best performance possible is expected from the students, but no more than that.

When tests are returned, answers and mistakes should be explained immediately. If necessary, review the directions or terms used in the test so that the students will be better prepared on the next test.

For those tests that are timed, provide the students with some experience in learning how to pace their work. This can be accomplished by playing a game that is timed or, for older students, timing them on completing a task.

Help students learn to pace their work by teaching them to look over the test first to see how much needs to be covered. Suggest to them that if they get stuck on a question to skip it and go on. Try the hard question later if there is time.

Many tests today are computer scored. It is beneficial to provide younger students, or students who have a visual-motor weakness, practice reading the question from one paper and filling in the answer on a second separate sheet. Also encourage them to use a ruler or other marker to keep their place as they record their answers.

It is also important to explain to students that *not* studying for a test creates inevitable and unacceptable stress.

Since tests are so universally used by teachers, an in-service workshop on test construction may help teachers construct better test instruments.

Homework

Assigning homework is probably better controlled in a self-contained classroom. Here only one teacher is assigning homework, so at least the amount assigned can be kept reasonable. In departmental systems, teachers often assign homework without regard for what others have assigned. This is true not only at the high school level but often into the middle grades as well. The assignment of homework assumes that all children can handle the assignment equally and that all children are equally capable—a process that argues against the individual differences concept.

Even when one teacher assigns the homework and presumably is aware of the students' capacities and functioning, stress can result. In one school system, students of a certain grade level are assigned one-half hour of work a night, and the work is assigned through agreement between the teachers who function on a departmental level. One student was given three pages of math to do and it took almost the entire thirty minutes just to copy the problems onto a piece of paper before they could be solved! Stress resulted from the feeling that since she was supposed to have one-half hour of homework a night and she couldn't do all the work in that time, then there must be something wrong with her!

Piling on homework often ensures a poor or mediocre result. Assigning homework for the sake of having homework is a waste of time and an insult to the students. They often feel it is nothing but busy work and they resent it. To use up a good portion of a student's time copying work from a book is equally resented.

Reducing stress There is little reason why homework cannot be coordinated to ensure that students are not overloaded. Although this may be easier at the elementary level than the junior and senior high, it is still possible and even desirable. More limited homework would hopefully result in homework with more meaning. Since less homework would be assigned, then perhaps teachers and students could focus on quality and meaningfulness. Instead of having students copy material from a book, make duplicates by using a copy machine. Homework could then be prepared, taking into consideration the students' needs, capacities, and skills.

Grades

Grades are usually assigned based on test results and work assignments. The assumption of grades is that all the children in the class are equally able to complete the work. Grades also assume that the material was well taught in a mode equally accepted by all students. Another assumption is that the tests used to measure teaching results are adequately constructed, and that the teacher and students agree on what material is important enough to be on the test. The fact that teachers often use grades to encourage, to stimulate, and even to punish, makes grades a source of great stress in children.

Reducing stress Grades should depend on evidence from many sources, not just from tests. Grades should be objectively assigned and should serve as a positive reinforcement. Taking a few minutes to explain why a certain grade is assigned will give a student the feeling he or she is valued regardless of the grade. Grades should be explained so that students can set appropriate goals for themselves based on their own strengths.

Promotion

In order to be promoted, children must pass tests that may not be adequately or fairly constructed; they must compete with other children for grades; they must alter their behavior to fit the expectations of teachers; their homework or assigned work must be done in the teacher's mode and to a teacher's satisfaction often without taking into consideration a student's learning style or problems; and they must adjust to a teacher's attitude and personality. Certainly the prospect of retention is a threat and a serious cause of stress for many students. Retention can also be seen as a form of punishment by the student who sees himself or herself working hard and trying his or her best. It is seldom seen as a failure of the teacher and school. The fact that retention often does little for a child psychologically and does little to enhance his or her learning should signal the school that other forms of teaching need to be applied before the child fails. Before and after retention, stress is high.

An example of a retention that failed is shown by a boy who was spending his third year in the seventh grade. Seen as "just lazy and a behavior problem," little was done for him. It was only after enrollment into a drop-out program that a learning disability was diagnosed. Unfortunately, the damage to his self-esteem was already accomplished.

It is our feeling that retention after the third grade does more harm than good.

Reducing stress Waiting until the end of the year and then suggesting retention is more a failure on the school's part than that of the student. Children should be helped to understand that some failure is normal. But to fail completely at the end of the school year is to fail the student as a person and not for some task he or she is unable to do.

Grouping

Most often, children are placed in groups within the class-room, usually based on a student's strengths and weaknesses. Grouping is achieved in the high school by the level of classes offered (honors, remedial, and so on). There are advantages and disadvantages to grouping. Stress is placed on children to the degree that they differ from the average for that grade, whether it be borderline IQ or gifted. The more they see they are different and the more differently they are treated, the greater the stress.

Reducing stress Grouping children is not a problem in and of itself. It is the results of grouping with which a teacher must be concerned. Grouping must keep a child's sense of self-worth intact. Children should know that all people have strengths and weaknesses and that grouping is an attempt at strengthening weaknesses and enhancing strengths.

Peer Pressure in the Classroom

Students who are new to a school or classroom are under the stressful situation of seeking acceptance by their peers. They must somehow find acceptance by meeting the stan-dards of the group, whatever that may be. If they cannot determine what these standards are or if they are unable to meet the standards, then they become loners and isolated. Adding to the stress is the desire to join a group whose values are in conflict with those of their parents. Even students who are not new to a classroom may feel stress when they do not meet the criteria for membership in a particular group.

Reducing stress Teachers can ease the acceptance of a new or unaccepted student by modeling. They must accept that child if they expect the child's peer group to do so. Finding strengths and weaknesses, likes and dislikes, as well as goals and aspirations of any student will allow the teacher to group that child appropriately, to involve that child in activities with children who have similar needs and interests.

Impossible Demands

Stress is often caused by teachers who place demands on students that cannot be met, or at least met to the teacher's standards. For example, a student may have poor handwriting yet must do papers over until they are what the teacher deems acceptable. Or assignments are given to such a degree that a student cannot keep up with the demand based upon his or her skills and ability. Some teachers use a "shotgun approach"; that is, they give everyone many assignments to keep them busy and expectations are the same for everyone.

Reducing stress Demands placed on students should be realistic and meaningful. The requirements made on a superior student will overwhelm a slower child. This is one of the problems with the "shotgun approach." Assignments should be made contingent upon the child's ability and capacity, and in a mode that enhances his or her learning rather than raising the student's stress level.

Length of Day

Many teachers recognize and accept that they work long hours, yet they do not give that same recognition to children. It is not unusual to have some children, high-school students in particular, arise at 5:30 to 6:00 in the morning to catch a school bus that arrives at school before classes start at 8:00

A.M. With classes over at 2:00 to 2:30, they then have a bus ride home, arriving at 3:00 to 3:30. Add to this the two to three hours of assigned work, and the student has already put in an eleven-hour day. When extracurricular activities and sports are included, it is not unusual for a student to have a fourteen- to fifteen-hour day. Long hours in school or school-related activities, responsibilities at home within the family, competing with other students, dealing with teachers and school staff, and living by varied sets of rules add to the stress.

Reducing stress The school day is often determined by state law, which states the number of hours that must be allocated to academic studies. Given these guidelines, it is difficult to adjust the school day.

Extracurricular Activities

Although many students gain from extracurricular activities, there are those who do not. Consider sports as an example. Of all the students who may wish to play baseball, for instance, only a selected few are chosen because they possess the necessary skills. This is repeated for all sports, thus excluding many individuals. Many students do not even attempt to go out for sports because of its selectiveness and because they feel certain they will be rejected. Apart from sports, there are other activities in which only selected students are sought, leaving out students who might be interested. There are students who are shy, who lack the time, who cannot affort the cost, who have other responsibilities, or who do not meet the standards. These are the students who feel stress because they cannot participate in activities in which they are interested, which then contributes to their loneliness and alienation.

Reducing stress Extracurricular activities should be open to all students as long as they are interested and willing to participate.

School Personnel

Apart from teachers and administrators, there are nurses, secretaries, clerks, custodians, and aides who interact with the students. How these people act toward the students can affect the students' stress level. There is certainly a difference in attitude between the custodian whose school held an "Appreciation Day" for him and the secretary who is avoided at all costs by the students. Some of these people engage in anger, insult, and sarcasm, and hold an inquisition at the least suspected behavior. Although children should have some anxiety and apprehension about any wrong doing, they should not feel fear and panic in facing any school employee. Sometimes, an explanation for an action taken by school personnel is all that is necessary to help a student accept the action.

Reducing stress   School personnel, other than teachers, often look upon their role in the school as merely a job, and little emphasis is placed on their interactions with students. Care must be taken by the administration that these people pursue their jobs with the philosophy of care and respect for the students. There is no reason why any staff member should resort to anger, sarcasm, or disrespect for any student while performing their job. A polite and pleasant manner goes a long way with children, as does a smile. Sometimes an explanation for a particular action or decision helps a student accept that action or decision. For example, recently my daughter and I stopped by the school to pick up a copy of the school menu for September. While I waited in the car, my daughter ran into the school and soon came out empty-handed. Although she was allowed to read the menu, the staff member would not give her a copy, nor was an explanation given. Why a "Top Secret" menu?

Competition

Unfortunately, competition and the pressure to do well are learned at an early age. The emphasis that some teachers place on competition and the need to finish first, sets up stress reactions in children and adolescents. The students then are fearful of not being able to meet the demands and expectations of the competition. Added to this is the possible loss of one's self-esteem and the loss of one's standing with peers. For some students, being asked to go to the chalkboard to struggle over a problem until it is solved is unbearable. The student may be urged to keep at it until a mistake is found. Spelling bees, math bees, power tests, and tests that demand rote completion of math facts within a sixty-second time period are typical competitions that occur within the classroom.

Reducing stress If competition is important to a teacher as a teaching tool, adjust the competition so that there is not one particular student or students that win consistently, or lose consistently. If power tests must be given, have the students mark where they were at a given time and permit them to finish the paper if they so desire. Reducing time pressures within the classroom aids the slower students. For those students with visual-motor difficulties, limiting the amount of written work lowers their stress. Use the chalkboard creatively. A student who is able to solve a problem successfully at the chalkboard will have an enhancement of their self-esteem when they are able to "instruct" their peers. Children and adolescents profit from demonstrating their strengths, not their weaknesses. It is also important to remember that although some anxiety enhances performance, too much anxiety lowers functioning.

The teacher and classroom stresses that have been discussed are not all-inclusive, nor are they present in all schools. It is hoped that many of the stress factors can at least be reduced and/or controlled, if not eliminated. Schools and teachers have the potential to enhance students' self-esteem and to provide the first alert to children's and adolescents' stresses. Most certainly, teachers are in a position to contribute positively to the mental health of students.

CHAPTER *7*

Signals of Depression

DEPRESSION

Depression, in general, is not the occasional feeling of being down or feeling blue. It is a serious illness and often a factor in suicide. Depression affects children and adolescents as well as adults. The following signs are not intended to be all-inclusive but an indication of signs typical of child and adolescent depression. The seriousness of any behavior must be evaluated in context of the child or adolescent, age, family environment, social environment, time duration, and general emotional adjustment.

Lack of Interest

The usual pleasant activities are no longer enjoyable for the child or adolescent. He or she loses interest in both academic and nonacademic activities and cannot be motivated. The person is easily bored or may complain a lot. He or she changes from being usually cooperative to being often hesitant or resistant to becoming involved. There is also the student who will disturb other students by his or her search for something that will be of interest. In general, depressed youths lack any enthusiasm for just about anything and there is often a change in attitude toward school and academics.

Possible classroom indicators The youth appears to be daydreaming or "cut off" from class discussions and/or activities. When work is finished quickly, it is sloppy and items are skipped or overlooked. On the other hand, if the student takes an unusually long time finishing work, the assignment may be incomplete or incorrect. The student may isolate herself or himself not only in the classroom but also socially. Slowness in physical movements may be noted. The student may draw, doodle, play, or handle objects listlessly. Very seldom will he or she volunteer to do anything. There may be disruptive behavior as the student is easily distracted, with poor attention and concentration. The student may "miss" directions or explanations.

Change in Appetite

The child or adolescent will pick at food and eat very little, complaining he or she is not hungry. Foods that are ordinarily enjoyed are no longer of interest. At the other extreme, the youth will not only eat his or her lunch but look to others for more food. Although not constantly hungry, the individual will eat whatever is available or continually want something to eat.

Possible classroom indicators A change in appetite is reflected by the child's or adolescent's increased appetite and concern about food or by a lack of appetite and disinterest in food. The important factor to note is the change from a previous behavior. The student might eat his or her lunch and then help others finish their lunch. Stealing lunches or snacks and/or borrowing money to buy additional lunches or snacks may also be components of the new behavior. Overall there seems to be a constant but vague need to be eating. On the other extreme, the student might begin giving away his or her lunch or most of it. When questioned, the youth will give various reasons why he or she isn't eating, ranging from "not hungry," to "have a stomachache," to "already full." The child or adolescent might listlessly push around food on a plate or tear a sandwich or bread into little pieces and roll them into balls. For some, there is a deliberate spoiling of the food. There is also an inability to pay attention or concentrate.

Change in Sleep Pattern

This may take the form of restless sleep, not being able to fall asleep at night, and/or waking up in the early morning hours unable to fall back to sleep. Excessive sleep may be another symptom. The former are the children and adolescents who come to school tired and with little energy. The excessive sleeper may be lethargic with little interest or motivation.

Possible classroom indicators Students might fall asleep in the classroom. There is much yawning, with listless and restless behavior. The energy level is low. Students display a lack of interest and avoid work and/or responsibility. They perhaps will miss school or be tardy because of oversleeping and will seldom do anything even when in the classroom. These students will lag behind everyone else. Poor attention and concentration are noted.

Loss of Energy

Some children and adolescents who are normally active and alert will show an apparent listlessness and tiredness. They may verbalize this loss of energy by complaining that they are too tired, they are not interested, or they are bored. In many cases there is no verbalizations—just behavior that shows a low energy level.

Possible classroom indicators Tired and/or restless behavior is seen with work not done or done too quickly. The student is sleepy or may fall asleep during class. Due to the lack of energy, he or she may put things off until tomorrow and become disorganized as things begin to pile up. When extra time is given to complete an assignment, the youth is unable to maintain an appropriate energy level to complete the task. He or she might be last to do everything and anything—last in line, last to lunch, last to put books/materials away, and so on. Again, there is poor attention and concentration.

Blaming Oneself Inappropriately

The child or adolescent takes the blame for everything that goes wrong. The youth will be generally self-depreciating, critical of his or her behavior and self, resulting in a negative self-concept.

Possible classroom indicators Withdrawn behavior or sullen behavior may be seen. The student may be defensive or passive. Usually the youth is self-critical, believing that he or she is different from peers. The person appears to have the weight of the world on his or her shoulders. Quick to react with tears to any kind of pressure, this student is an easy target for others to pick on because he or she lacks confidence. The youth is extremely sensitive and a worrier. He or she may appear "touchy" and fretful, and is upset by surprises or changes from the routine. Often the person believes he or she will not be accepted by the teacher, or will take criticism personally as though there is something wrong with him or her. The youth will be inconsolable, holding on to a hurt and/or talking under his or her breath. There may also be poor attention and concentration.

Negative Feelings of Self-Worth

Negative feelings in children and adolescents are reflected in feelings of worthlessness. They feel as though they are unloved and unwanted by everyone. Relationships with others tend to be poor since they often feel used. There is social withdrawal since these youths feel unworthy of any positive relationships and feel incapable of maintaining long-term relationships. They feel a general inability to be liked and accepted.

Possible classroom indicators This passive student does not stand up for himself or herself and is afraid to say "no." There is poor peer relationships and there may be teasing by peers. For the student who attempts to cover up feelings of worthlessness, there is an air of defensiveness. He or she may be critical of others, quick to point out the mistakes or misbehaviors of others. The student needs emotional support from the teacher. Overall, there may be poor classroom achievement with difficulty in paying attention and concentrating.

Feelings of Sadness, Hopelessness, and Worry

Children and adolescents with these feelings look and feel unhappy. There are feelings of rejection and feelings of helplessness in dealing with life circumstances. They appear withdrawn and inhibited as well as fearful. They worry not only about themselves but about things they have little control over.

Possible classroom indicators The child or adolescent looks and feels sad and unhappy. He or she gives up easily and needs encouragement to attempt and complete assigned work. The student may be disorganized due to the inability to concentrate or pay attention to what is going on in the classroom. If mistakes are pointed out, the student tends to feel overwhelmed when required to make the corrections. The youth feels that he or she cannot do anything right and believes that his or her classwork and/or personality will never be accepted by others. He or she may feel unable to do an assignment that has previously been successfully completed. The youth feels defeat and/or failure before even getting started. These children or adolescents may feel disturbed by everything, not just a specific issue. There are poor peer relationships and the children or adolescents act frightened. There is a need for emotional support from the teacher.

Inability to Concentrate or Attend

Poor attentive abilities are often reflected in daily assignments in the classroom as well as in a general decline or drop in school grades. The youth has difficulty focusing attention onto school work, or anything else, since his or her thought process is being disrupted by fears and concerns.

Possible classroom indicators The child or adolescent takes a long time to complete or may not complete work, and is easily distracted. Assignments or books are forgotten or can't be found. Attention span is very short and thinking is "scattered"; responsibilities are often forgotten. The youth has difficulty working independently, following directions, and may appear not to be listening. He or she interrupts with questions and/or often interrupts with a question that the teacher may be answering at the moment. Immediately after instructions are given, the child or adolescent asks to have them repeated, saying that he or she didn't understand. Some questions will not even be related to the subject matter. Because of disorganization and felt anxiety, the student may be constantly in motion which in and of itself is disorganized.

Morbid Thoughts

Children and adolescents are normally not concerned with death to a point where they dwell on it. Depressed youngsters will often have thoughts of death and/or suicide to an excessive degree.

Possible classroom indicators The student may be fearful and overreact to someone's death. He or she talks or writes with morbid death themes, or it may be evident in art work. There is an overinvolvement or excitement concerning terrorists or war actions. The student, on more than one occasion and within a short time period, selects materials that deal with death, dying, suicide, or worthlessness of life.

MASKED DEPRESSION

Some professionals hold the view that childhood depression is different from the adult depressive disorders. In this view, the symptoms are "masked," that is, the depression is shown through symptoms that are not necessarily associated with or identified with depression. The rationale behind masked depression is that the depressed feelings are replaced by behavior problems (Clarizio, 1982). Although there is some controversy surrounding this concept, we believe there is sufficient reason to consider aggressive or negative behavior, increased agitation, increased psychosomatic complaints, decreased academic performance, and poor attention and concentration as possible masked depressive behaviors.

Aggressive or Negative Behaviors

The youngster will show generally aggressive or negative behavior, both in and out of the classroom.

Possible classroom indicators   The child or adolescent might pick on others and experience peer difficulties. He or she may become aggressive with others, yell, throw objects, and react quickly at the first hint of trouble. If articulate, the student may talk back and be verbally aggressive. The typical response to all interactions is negative and even perhaps physical. There is disruptive behavior both in and out of the classroom. It seems that the student seeks any and every opportunity to challenge or confront. He or she may even refuse punishment and doesn't seem to care about the consequences. There is an attitude of being defeated before one starts. The student may sometimes appear afraid to attempt school assignments. Overall, there is a low frustration tolerance.

Increased Agitation

The child's or adolescent's overall physical activity is increased. He or she cannot sit still and there is an agitation to movements. The youth is overinvolved and has difficulty completing any task.

Possible classroom indicators The child or adolescent has a short attention span, is easily distracted, is restless, and cannot sit still. There is a low frustration tolerance, with a quick reaction either verbally or physically. He or she has difficulty staying on task, having several projects going at once but seldom completing any of them. The student will miss directions and then interrupt the teacher to ask questions that were previously explained, or will ask unnecessary questions and/or make unnecessary comments. The youth is frequently out of his or her seat and will say the wrong thing at the wrong time due to a lack of attention. He or she may make noises in the classroom and/or talk under his or her breath.

Increased Psychosomatic Complaints

The child or adolescent frequently complains of not feeling well.

Possible classroom indicators Headaches, stomachaches, sore muscles, and/or other vague comments of just not feeling well are frequent complaints. There are frequent visits to the school nurse or health aide. The student will put his or her head down on the desk even before class starts. This student seeks constant attention but doesn't demand it. At times, the student may have a "lost puppy stance" and follow the teacher around continuously. There is a lack of attention and concentration. The youth may have patterns of frequent absences of short duration. These absences are often due to psychosomatic complaints.

Decreased Academic Performance

The child or adolescent is functioning below expected grade level.

Possible classroom indicators Typically, independent work and homework assignments are poorly done. There is poor test performance due to lack of preparation and inattentiveness. The student either dawdles over the work or is overly quick to finish it. He or she appears disorganized and may have a messy desk. There is an avoidance of responsibility; often assignments and supplies are "forgotten." The student is indecisive, has a limited attention span, and has poor concentration. There may be a drop in grades (e.g., an A/B student now earns grades of C/D).

Poor Attention and Concentration

The child or adolescent cannot attend to tasks or focus attention appropriately.

Possible classroom indicators The student takes an unusually long time to finish assignments or when work is quickly finished, items may be skipped. There is disruptive behavior due to an inability to stay on task. Frequent interruptions are necessary because the student misses directions. He or she seeks attention from teacher and peers, which results in wasting class time. Materials, assignments, and responsibilities are forgotten. The student falls farther behind in class and work assignments every day. Usually the student sits in class and does nothing. Excessive daydreaming may be noted.

In conclusion, signs of depression may fit all students at one time or another, but it is the change in behavior and the duration of that behavior that is important. If any abrupt change occurs in a student and this deviation lasts approximately two weeks or longer, referral to the appropriate personnel for further investigation is recommended.

Signals of Depression

1. Lack of interest
2. Change in appetite

3. Change in sleep pattern
4. Loss of energy
5. Blaming oneself inappropriately
6. Negative feelings of self-worth
7. Feelings of sadness, hopelessness, and worry
8. Inability to concentrate or attend
9. Morbid thoughts

Signals of Masked Depression

10. Aggressive or negative behaviors
11. Increased agitation
12. Increased psychosomatic complaints
13. Decreased academic performance
14. Poor attention and concentration

CHAPTER **8**

Signals of Suicide

Recognizing when a youth is at risk for a suicide is difficult because many of the symptoms appear to be common teenage behaviors. The youth who is at risk pushes erratic behavior to the extreme.

This chapter will list and discuss the signals of suicide and provide specifics of what to look for. Whereas the signals of suicide and depression overlap, it is important to keep in mind that there is no one complete list for any child or adolescent, whether it be for depression or suicide. Suicide is never as simple as a single cause. It is usually a very complicated combination of social, emotional, and personal factors to which biological factors may be added.

SUICIDE ALERT LIST FOR CHILDREN AND ADOLESCENTS

A Previous Suicide Attempt

Any previous attempt at suicide should be a signal that some intervention should be undertaken.

Possible classroom indicators None. The teacher's awareness of a past attempt should, however, warrant a referral to appropriate school personnel.

✶A Threat of Suicide

Statements such as "I'm going to kill myself," "I can't take it anymore," "People would be better off without me," should be taken seriously and the reason for such statements should be investigated. These are statements of extreme frustration and concern, signaling a loss of hope with possibly nowhere to turn except suicide.

Possible classroom indicators A teacher hearing the above type statements should discuss them with the student. Many times students will convey their feelings and thoughts in their writings. Any overly depressing or morbid writings should be investigated with the student. Any concern that the child or adolescent is experiencing stress or problems should be followed with a referral to appropriate school personnel.

✶ Feelings of Hopelessness and Helplessness

Often children and adolescents lead lives or encounter situations that are basically detrimental to their mental health. Since they are often powerless to change or influence the course of their lives or resolve specific circumstances, they develop overpowering feelings of hopelessness. Seeing no resolution to their problems, their solution is suicide.

Possible classroom indicators Children and adolescents with these feelings appear withdrawn, inhibited, and fearful. They look and feel unhappy. They give up easily and do not become involved since they feel powerless to influence anything. Frequent comments are "I can't," "It doesn't matter," "What difference does it make?" and "Why bother?" These children and adolescents develop "tunnel vision." They can only see one solution, usually suicide, to their problem. They fail to take into consideration any alternative solutions, even when offered to them.

Talk of Death or Despair or a Preoccupation with Thoughts of Death

This sign indicates that death has become a strong force in the students' thinking patterns and perhaps one which frightens them. They need to have someone with whom they can share their concerns and help in breaking the thought pattern.

Possible classroom indicators Any unusual interest in death, as evidenced through discussions and/or papers, themes, or art work, should be of concern and discussed with the student and/or appropriate school personnel. One type of theme that is overlooked by many as a suicide indicator is an overinvolvement with thoughts of war and terrorist and/ or suicide missions.

Anxiety and Tension

Although anxiety and tension are symptoms of many behavior patterns, they are of more serious consequence in suicide, especially if one sees them coupled with other signs of suicide.

Possible classroom indicators Obvious signs of stress and tension are exhibited by little patience with self or others, withdrawal from usual social contacts, lowered classroom performance (i.e., poorly done assignments or poor test results), poor attention, and poor concentration.

Withdrawal from Family and Friends

Some children and adolescents act out their unhappiness so it can be seen, but some withdraw into themselves. They slowly cut themselves off from everyone. They often withdraw from family due to guilt or anger over their feelings and behaviors or just by virtue of their negative self-concept. They don't wish to burden their family or friends with their feelings and problems. These children and adolescents often fear getting angry, perhaps for fear of losing control. Suppressing this anger simply intensifies it until finally they act on it, often by suicide. Our feelings are that these are the youngsters of greatest risk and who need to be reached quickly.

Possible classroom indicators The students exhibit quiet and withdrawn behavior that was not previously present. There is no participation in class discussion, along with an avoidance of groups and group participation. The youths may procrastinate, and homework assignments are poorly done, if at all. Poor attention and concentration are apparent. If questioned, the youths will make up any kind of excuse, usually "I forgot" or "I don't know." These adolescents and children appear to be daydreaming or off in another world. Physical movements are slowed down. It appears to be an effort to even get out the classroom door when leaving the classroom.

Violent and/or Rebellious Behavior

Some children and adolescents will act out their feelings rather than try to resolve them by constructively dealing with them. They simply get rid of any feelings they have through acting-out behavior. They may be involved in petty crime, show violent behavior, run away from home and/or school, or involve themselves in generally antisocial behavior as a way of coping with their feelings. Acting-out behaviors are often seen as normal, especially for boys, but the extent and magnitude may signal a loss of control such as that seen in suicide.

Possible classroom indicators Acting-out behaviors can be demonstrated both verbally and physically. There may be verbal and/or physical abuse of others, theft, and lack of respect for others or their property. Often these youths respond negatively to authority. They are frequently in and out of their seat and may pester or pick on other students. They interrupt and may be loud and obnoxious. There is no delay mechanism on behavior and so the youths may try to gratify all desires immediately and perhaps even crudely. These students may write on desks, tear pages out of books, and mutilate equipment and/or lockers. They appear to be withdrawn and could be described as "removed from their environment." The youth doesn't smile or laugh and appears to be mad at the world. There may be a "chip-on-the-shoulder" attitude. Overall, inattentiveness in the classroom is exhibited.

Drug and/or Alcohol Abuse

Drug and alcohol abuse is seen by some as a slow form of suicide. Certainly it is a signal of a youth's inability to cope with the stresses of reality and often a withdrawal into themselves. Many adolescents who commit suicide have had drugs and alcohol shortly before their deaths. A large amount of alcohol drunk and/or drugs used before committing suicide tempers the fear of death. In addition, alcohol and/or drugs will often deepen aggression, which, if turned inward towards oneself, may result in suicide (Griffin and Felsenthal, 1983).

Possible classroom indicators Behaviors can either be withdrawn or acting out. There is a lack of attention and concentration or, as some students call it, a "mellowing out" with unusual highs or lows. Depending upon the substance used, there may also be red eyes, dilated pupils, a runny nose, and hoarseness.

Giving Away Valued Possessions or Making Final Arrangements

These are usually more apparent signs that a person may be contemplating suicide. The making of final arrangements can take various forms, from giving away valued possessions to making a will entrusted to a "good friend."

Possible classroom indicators None. However, any knowledge that a teacher gains from the student or other students that a child or adolescent is making final arrangements should result in some discussion with that student or a referral to appropriate school personnel.

Abrupt Changes in Behavior

Changes in mood are not unexpected in children and adolescents, or for adults. But abrupt and prolonged changes in behavior may be cause for concern. There are usually reasons for someone to go from being happy to being moody, from outgoing to withdrawal, from passive to aggressive, and from concern to lethargy. These reasons may be temporary and transient, or of a serious enough nature to be a factor in suicide.

Possible classroom indicators Look for behaviors and/or academic performance that are opposite of what is expected for that student. For example, be alert to a student who was previously outgoing who becomes withdrawn. Such a student may have previously chatted easily with the teacher but now ducks out of the classroom to avoid even the most casual teacher or peer contact. Once interested in various school activities, the student may now lack involvement in any activities. He or she will also have a short attention span.

Sudden, Unexplicable Euphoric or Whirlwind Activity after a Period of Depression

This sign could mean that the youth has come to a decision to take the fatal step. Indecision often contributes to anxiety and depression, and once a decision is made—positive or negative—some relief is felt. In this case, the decision may have been made to commit suicide and thus relief is felt over having made that decision.

Possible classroom indicators After a period of with-drawn or "down" behavior, these students suddenly become talkative, excited, and sometimes boisterous and loud. Once able to contain themselves, now they simply cannot sit still or concentrate. There is a constant "fiddling" with any object that comes to hand. These youths might begin one activity or assignment only to quickly begin another without ever finishing the first, or the activity or assignment may be rushed through with many careless errors.

Running Away from Home

Children and adolescents give a variety of reasons for running away from home. Usually, in their minds, the reasons are reasonable and legitimate, ranging from what they see as unfair restrictions to serious abuse. Running away suggests some problems within the family unit as well as within the child or adolescent. Often running away is seen as a last resort and also serves notice that the youngster finds the situation at home or school intolerable. If the situation is not resolved at least to some degree then the child or adolescent may see no other alternative but suicide.

Possible classroom indicators Real or even imagined crises at school may precipitate the running-away behavior. Typically runaways have lower grades, difficulty in interacting with teachers and peers, less involvement with the support system of extracurricular activities, and higher absenteeism (Berkovitz, 1985).

Change in School and Academic Performance

Most children and adolescents do not function consistently in school. They have normal highs and lows, successes and failures. There are subjects they like and subjects they dislike. Changes in school and academic performance for those children who have a high degree of concern seem to affect their general functioning and occur usually over a period of time. A usually good student begins to fail; he or she misses school more regularly; assignments are late and/or poorly done or not handed in at all; and his or her attitude towards school turns negative. These are signs saying that the child or adolescent doesn't care. These youths are preoccupied with other thoughts or things that are of greater priority. They have other issues that need to be resolved. Taken to an extreme and coupled with other factors, suicide may be a way of dealing with all their failures. This may be especially true for learning-disabled students. A pilot study of fourteen suicide victims in Los Angeles County found that 50% of the individuals were learning disabled (Berkovitz, 1985).

Boredom

Most people go through periods of boredom from time to time, but when it becomes the rule rather than the exception then it may deserve concern. It would seem in this day and age of electronics and computers that there are ample activities to keep children and adolescents from getting bored. In spite of all there is to stimulate the mind and body, children and adolescents frequently complain of being bored and many expect someone or something to entertain them. Perhaps boredom is a factor in the increased use of drugs and alcohol in our adolescent populations as well as accounting in part for the epidemic of teenage pregnancies. At any rate, to see children and adolescents in a constant state of boredom when there is so much to stimulate them suggests a withdrawal or inability to adjust to life in general. Being out of step with their peers has been a factor in more than a few suicides.

Possible classroom indicators Not only are these students easily distracted but they distract other students. Work is finished quickly or not at all, and materials and books are often forgotten. There may be an attitude of "Do whatever you like. It doesn't matter to me." These students don't accept responsibility. Along with poor attention and concentration, there is a restlessness. There may be some involvement with drugs/alcohol, with some noticeable reaction in the classroom.

Inability to Concentrate

The ability to concentrate depends on one's capacity to focus on one train of thought to the exclusion of interfering thoughts. Children and adolescents who are upset enough to contemplate suicide are constantly dealing with and attempting to analyze and weigh many thoughts and feelings related to self. Because of the hurt and pain they feel, they are often dealing with conflicting feelings and emotions, trying to put everything into focus. For them to focus and concentrate on any one issue, especially academics, is impossible since their attempts to deal with their emotions take a higher priority.

Possible classroom indicators These adolescents and children may be viewed as daydreamers. They are easily distracted, lose their place frequently, have the wrong book/assignment, are inattentive, and are often late. If work is completed, it has been rushed through and is usually of poor quality. Written assignments may take longer than usual to complete. The students may have trouble starting tasks. Disorganized and needing help, they are often viewed as wasting the teacher's time as well as their peers' time. These youths are thinking about many things and are often viewed as forgetful, especially when it comes to responsibilities. When questioned about the forgetfulness, they will usually say "sorry" with no explanation. An overdependency on others seems to develop in some students.

Feelings of Worthlessness

Many children and adolescents who think of suicide have feelings of worthlessness and, perhaps, hatred for themselves. They measure themselves against other significant people in their lives and usually fall short of their own expectations. They magnify their weaknesses and avoid emphasizing their strengths because they don't recognize or believe they have any strengths. Some children and adolescents who have these feelings of worthlessness may try to cover them up so that no one else will know that they're "not any good."

Possible classroom indicators   There may be withdrawn behavior and a lack of confidence. These students may cry easily and react strongly to even the slightest criticism. Typically they turn in assigned work that is poorly done. If asked to make corrections, they may ignore or even repeat the same errors. Socially, the youths may tend to associate with younger children. Sometimes they become upset both physically and mentally as they fume and fret too much and tend to get moody. These students have difficulty with change in a routine and/or cannot handle surprises easily.

For those children and adolescents who try to cover up their feelings of worthlessness, there may be tendencies toward trying to make themselves look more superior by making others look inferior. Other cover-up tactics might be sarcasm, attention-seeking behavior, or behavior that might at first be thought of as competitive but upon reflection is more imposition and confrontation. There may also be laughter and talking at inappropriate times.

Physical Complaints

Children and adolescents with chronic illnesses are probably more prone to depression than the average. Children without chronic illnesses who are depressed will often complain of vague physical symptoms that cannot be verified or diagnosed.

Possible classroom indicators   There are frequent complaints for minor aches and pains along with repeated requests to visit the school nurse and frequent absences. The older children and adolescents may "self-doctor" openly in the classroom. The younger children tend to follow the teacher around or be at the teacher's desk frequently, asking that the teacher look at small scratches, scrapes, and bumps. The teacher may even be unaware that the child is there until the teacher looks up and finds the student beside him or her.

Changes in Sleeping Patterns

Changes in children's and adolescents' sleeping habits may be seen in different ways. They may start sleeping for longer periods of time or not sleep much at all; they may not sleep at regular times but at odd hours. Sleep may also be easily disturbed so the end result is that of being exhausted. Over a period of time, this pattern may result in physical and/or psychological problems because natural defenses have been weakened.

Possible classroom indicators Students may voice complaints of being tired and sleepy. Some may even fall asleep during class and the teacher may have difficulty waking them. Achievement is down because the youths miss so much school, and even when present in class, they may not know what is going on. There is an obvious difficulty in attending and concentrating, which might be accompanied by overt restlessness. These students seldom complete assignments or volunteer to do anything in the classroom because they have no energy. During recess or lunch, they may withdraw to avoid any participation that might require any expenditure of physical or psychic energies.

Recent Suicide of Someone Close or Someone with Whom They Identify

It is presently thought that a person is more likely to commit suicide if there has been a suicide in his or her family. Also, those who are already contemplating suicide may be encouraged to complete it by the suicide of someone they know, like, or admire. Since children and adolescents identify so closely with friends as well as with popular personalities from movies and television shows, suicide by any of these may bring them closer to making their own attempt. Many times suicide victims are glamorized by their schools and the media. This affects others who are fragile and vulnerable. They view this recognition and attention obtained by suicide as something that is very appealing.

Possible classroom indicators Children and adolescents will overfocus on the morbid and depressing, with references to death. Although this overfocusing can occur in any class, English teachers in particular are often given clues about suicidal youths by their creative writings and discussions. Again, there is notable poor attention and concentration.

Changes in Eating Habits

The present emphasis on physical fitness can be expected to influence children and adolescents and their eating habits. Within limits, this is normal. However, serious eating disorders such as bulimia and anorexia nervosa or periods of starvation and binge eating are certainly problem signs. Any sudden change in eating habits should be cause for concern.

Possible classroom indicators There is either an avoidance or an overinvolvement with food. Youths will not eat snacks or lunch, or will consume theirs and help others finish their lunches. Those students who are avoiding food will give away their lunch or most of it. Those who are overly concerned with food will steal lunches or snacks. Within the classroom, there is poor attention and concentration.

Abrupt Changes in School Attendance

School officials need to be alert to those students with a good to average school attendance record who begin to have excessive absences. A commonly occurring situation prior to a suicide is that students will be involved in a school-related crisis (Stanley and Barter, 1970; Teicher and Jacobs, 1966).

Possible classroom indicators Students with average to good attendance records will abruptly begin to have excessive absenteeism. When questioned, they will have countless reasons for missing school, ranging from being sick, to oversleeping, to parents needing the student at home. Achievement is down because these youths miss so much school. Even when in school, they often are so far behind that it is impossible to catch up on the work. These children and adolescents are unaware of what is going on in the classroom. Although they are present in body, they are mentally absent.

In conclusion, although most people who attempt and/or complete suicide do give signs of their intention, they may give different signs to different people, thereby never allowing one person the opportunity to put all the signs together. This emphasizes the importance of acting on *any* sign given by children and adolescents that they may be contemplating suicide.

Signals of Suicide

1. A previous suicide attempt
2. A threat of suicide
3. Feelings of hopelessness and helplessness
4. Talk of death or despair or a preoccupation with thoughts of death
5. Anxiety and tension
6. Withdrawal from family and friends
7. Violent and/or rebellious behavior
8. Drug and/or alcohol abuse
9. Giving away valued possessions or making final arrangements
10. Abrupt changes in behavior
11. Sudden, unexplicable euphoric or whirlwind activity after a period of depression
12. Running away from home
13. Change in school and academic performance
14. Boredom
15. Inability to concentrate
16. Feelings of worthlessness
17. Physical complaints
18. Changes in sleeping patterns

19. Recent suicide of someone close or someone with whom they identify
20. Changes in eating habit
21. Abrupt changes in school attendance

Section Three

Section Three contains guidelines for establishing programs in suicide prevention, suicide intervention, and postvention. There are also general suggestions for working with children and adolescents in preventing suicide and in dealing with the aftermaths of suicide.

CHAPTER 9

Suicide Prevention in the Schools

It is necessary for our schools to plan, develop, organize, and implement a program in suicide prevention. This chapter will present an overview of global and specific concepts pertinent to a suicide prevention program.

There are a number of elements in a school suicide prevention program that must be addressed if the program is to be successful and effective.

1. The Board of Education must set up a school system-wide policy on suicide prevention, which will be administered by the Superintendent of Schools.
2. Focus on the social and emotional tone set by all schools and develop a positive and healthy mental health influence.
3. Ensure that there is a sufficient number of staff and faculty to carry out the proposed or adopted plan.
4. Increase awareness of the suicide prevention, intervention, and postvention programs in order to promote acceptance and cooperation of faculty, staff, and students.
5. Organize the suicide prevention program.

6. Organize a specific intervention program. (See Chapter 10.)
7. Organize a specific postvention program. (See Chapter 11.)

DEVELOPMENT OF THE SUICIDE PREVENTION PROGRAM

I. BOARD OF EDUCATION POLICY

Being in a position of educational leadership in the community, a school policy on suicide prevention would call attention to the schools and to the community the serious nature of suicide in our children and adolescents. By adopting a policy on suicide, the school board would publicly announce that it intends to provide for sufficient funds and staff to implement the program. To do otherwise would imply little or no support for the program, thus resulting in the same attitudes and feelings from school staff and community.

To attempt to implement a program without school board support leaves each school to their own plan and program, using whatever funds and staff are available. It also results in different programs aimed at specific groups or age levels when, in reality, one program should be implemented on a school-wide basis. The program should be started in the early grades and continue through high school, adapted to the intellectual, social, and emotional levels of the children involved. When programs are short term and keyed only to one or two specific groups, they tend to have minimal impact on students because they are usually symptom related. That is, they focus on behaviors of the present usually without considering long-term development and causes of the specific behaviors.

The policy should simply state that is the intent of the school board, schools, and staff to prevent suicide; that they recognize suicidal intent as indicative of serious underlying problems; and that every effort will be made to offer and provide help and assistance. This help and assistance should include early identification; support and/or counseling by school support personnel for low-risk students; referral to appropriate sources outside the school for high- and moderate-risk students; attendance to the rights of the student and his or her family; aftercare support by the school; and aftercare support for faculty, staff, and students after a sudden death has occurred.

In lieu of Board policy, or when a Board is hesitant or slow in acting, individual schools should set up guidelines for dealing with a crisis. These guidelines could follow those suggested in this book, using available school personnel.

II. SOCIAL AND EMOTIONAL TONE OF THE SCHOOL

A. Mental Health of Faculty

It is often said that one can feel the tone of a school just by entering it. There is little doubt that the quietness or noisiness, the order or chaos will give a visitor a feeling for the school atmosphere. That atmosphere is often set by the principal through her or his administration but also by the attitudes the teachers, staff, and students have developed.

Perhaps the best way of improving the emotional climate of schools is to improve the mental health of the faculty and staff since they primarily control the functioning of the school. One obvious but long-term method is to screen applicants carefully for teaching positions. More emphasis must be placed on the teacher as a person, along with his or her teaching skills.

A second way of enhancing the mental health of the school and the teacher is to improve working conditions. Teachers' salaries are still low as compared to other professionals, although they are beginning to improve. Teaching load and school responsibilities are still such that they take away from the teacher-student relationship. Teachers are often so bogged down with administrative responsibilities that they have little time to devote to the students' needs and problems. Special personnel are often handicapped by poor and inadequate materials and facilities and a high caseload.

A third way of developing positive mental health is to make services available to teachers that will help them with their personal problems. Teachers, as well as students, are not beyond suicide if their problems extend beyond their abilities to cope. Their coping skills are directly related to their state of mental health.

Although most teachers are covered by insurance programs that pay, in part, for mental health services, the insurance is generally inadequate and does not cover common areas of concern such as marriage counseling or sex therapy. Very often the problems teachers have do not need in-depth psychological intervention. They simply need an understanding person who can help them just by listening or by assisting them in making decisions. A long overdue concept is an Employees Assistance Program (EAP). This program can help teachers resolve issues before they become too involved or, if already serious, can lead teachers to appropriate outside sources. The results of such a program can lead to a teacher's better mental health, thereby improving the emotional tone of the school. An EAP can also aid in keeping health insurance costs at a reasonable level.

The following suggestions are more immediate ways of enhancing positive mental health in the schools.

1. *Recognition* Implement a program of giving recognition to teachers and staff for their work and contributions. Many teachers have new and innovative ways of teaching material to children, yet they and their techniques are not recognized nor encouraged. If the techniques are successful, they need to be shared with other teachers. The recognition does not have to be system wide but only from those in supervisory positions. System-wide recognition is certainly to be encouraged, but the point is that schools should give immediate support and recognition to successful teachers. Teachers, like other professionals, need to feel successful in their roles and functions. Success enhances positive mental health, thereby allowing teachers to react in a positive sense to the problems of students.

2. *Inservice workshops* Workshops in appropriate areas will help enhance teachers' skills. Unfortunately, teachers often resist the inservice workshop concept, perhaps because attendance is mandatory and the workshops are not timely. We suggest that teachers be treated as the professionals they are, requiring from them a minimum number of certified hours of growth and development a year, and allowing them to pick appropriate activities. The school could continue to offer inservice programs based on teacher interest, but not mandated by the administration.

3. *Workshops and conferences* There are numerous teacher workshops and conferences being held daily. However, many teachers are not allowed or are discouraged from attending either by restrictive leave policies or limited money budgeted for that purpose. An example is one school system that allots $75.00 a year for a workshop for an entire department. This allows one workshop a year, if that, for one person that is fortunate enough to have been selected, with choice based on cost not interest. Some school systems also limit the number of conference days allowed. An example is one school system that allows only one conference day per year. Conferences that last more than one day or are at a distance are thus eliminated. We advocate a more liberal policy for workshop attendance, not only for those dealing with serious learning/behavior problems but for teachers to enhance their general teaching skills.

B. Mental Health of Students

Mental health issues and mental health wellness should be an integral part of every school's health curriculum. Often overlooked as a possible prevention source, a school's health program could help students become aware of the signals and behavioral and verbal actions of a peer at risk. Equally as important, issues such as confidentiality and responsibilities could be discussed, as well as where to go to ask for advice or help.

1. *Student workshops* Students at all levels could benefit in both learning and mental health by being allowed to attend inservice workshops at the school. Areas of interest and need could easily be determined and workshops that are run by qualified professionals could be offered. Focusing these workshops toward all grade levels would be a good source of learning about social skills, problem solving, stress management, drugs and alcohol, sex, and so on. It most certainly would be a unique and innovative way of conducting a school day!

2. *Discussion groups* Time in the classroom should be allowed and encouraged for general discussion groups on topics of growth, development, emotions, social skills, depression, suicide, drugs and alcohol, and so on. These discussions would not only allow children a valuable learning opportunity but would encourage the strengthening of ties between children and teacher. Certainly, positive relationships between teacher and student should be encouraged. These discussions should be allowed with the understanding that the teachers are equipped to handle the topic and with available resources such as school mental health workers and outside consultants.

3. *Stress reduction* Areas of stress and suggestions for reducing stress are discussed in Chapters 6 and 12. Teaching students to recognize stress and, more importantly, learning how to reduce stress could begin as early as kindergarten and continue throughout a child's educational career. The cumulative effect of day-to-day stresses that are not handled appropriately can wear an individual down and create a tendency toward depression for some of the more vulnerable students. Classroom strategies for stress reduction can be built into a daily routine. The benefits of taking five minutes from the day's schedule to reduce stress are too numerous to list, but one very important merit is that once children are taught how to reduce stress they will utilize the strategies in later settings and situations.

There are many stress-reduction strategies on the market that can be adapted for use with children. Basically, stress reduction teaches one how to recognize tension, both mental and physical, and how to utilize visualization exercises. Examples of stress-reduction strategies are given in Chapter 12.

4. *Pressure and competition* Pressure and competition should be exerted only to the degree students can effectively deal with it. Students and teachers function better when the pressure put on them is within their means to handle. This certainly suggests looking at students and teachers as individuals, not as a large group with the same or even similar needs and capacities. Take a closer look at homework, tests, projects, papers, and sports and make them more appropriate for the student. One assignment for all students is generally unfair. Overall, realistic and positive expectations will lead to greater success for most students.

5. *Value clarification and problem solving* In our modern and complex society, children are continuously bombarded with conflicting messages. There are varying messages from parents and family units, the advertising world, peers, and the schools themselves. What seems to be occurring for some of our youths is an absorption of confusion, of values and ideas that seem to conflict with one another. Children are not only left without any clear guidelines but without any idea of how to problem solve and clarify ideas and values.

Values have been taught in some schools for many years but never on a consistent basis or in a planned curriculum. The schools worry if children cannot read or do arithmetic and may even worry about the students' honesty, helpfulness, and responsibility, however, little is done to enhance the latter areas. Serious consideration should be given to a planned curriculum for teaching values agreed upon by the school and community. It is our contention that helping a child or adolescent learn appropriate values and reinforcing the use of those values will lead to better adjusted individuals with good self-esteem. This cannot but help lower the use of suicide as a coping mechanism. Chapter 12 provides some guidelines for work in these areas.

6. *Social skill building*   A youth who has poor peer relationships due to inadequate social skills receives reinforcement that he or she is inadequate. This feeling of inadequacy confirms and increases within the youth his or her feelings of low self-esteem, isolation, and depression. Suggestions for working with students who have marginal social skills are included in Chapter 12.

Bloomquist (1974) has several good suggestions for developing an atmosphere of good mental health. Among them are to encourage children to participate in extracurricular and community service activities as a deterrent to withdrawal and isolation, and to include in the curriculum a more positive study of society that stresses problem solving. He also suggests that attempts be made to see that all students have at least one friend, and that schools allow counselors to counsel instead of performing administrative duties.

III. FACULTY AND STAFF

Many schools do not have an adequate number of staff, whether they be teachers or support personnel. Large classes are still the rule rather than the exception. To enhance a teacher's mental health, to provide for better individual and small group instruction, and to allow for a warmer, more personal relationship between teacher and student, small groups are essential. The fact that many suicidal students feel alone and alienated should be ample reason for closer student-teacher relationships.

Students who have problems, which could possibly be dealt with by the teacher in a small class with in-house consultation available, are often referred to special service personnel who are also understaffed. Not only are they understaffed but they are often at odds as to role and function. The school psychologist, the counselor, and the social worker have overlapping functions and should be encouraged to work together as a team for the mutual benefit of all students. One of the problems that must be corrected is the expectation for special personnel to provide services for which they are not trained. For example, many school psychology programs have only a small component of their program in counseling, yet school psychologists are seen as able to handle almost any type of problem. School counselors have strong vocational/academic training, yet they are also called upon to counsel students with serious problems. Even the school nurse takes on a counseling role in some school systems. What must be emphasized and encouraged is sufficient, adequately trained staff.

IV. ACCEPTANCE AND COOPERATION

A. Staff and Students

A successful program needs the acceptance and cooperation of both staff and students. Programs that are forced on teachers and students are often met with hostility and uncooperativeness. Any program or plan to deal with suicide should encourage the cooperation of interested teachers and students within their availability and capacities. Most teachers have a realistic view of their students' capacities, needs, and expectations. They are more in tune with how those children learn and what they respond to at different levels. To not take advantage of this expertise is to tempt a less than successful program. Students as part of the program planning can give insight as to the best approaches to use with their peers. They can pin down areas of specific interest and concern. The fact that many youths who commit or attempt suicide confide in their friends suggests that students are in a unique position to prevent or intervene in a suicide, given the proper knowledge and understanding.

A program in which both teachers and students are involved stands a greater chance of success since there is ego involvement. That is, both sides need to feel success not only as competent people in their own right, but as competent and successful people in the eyes of others.

B. Parents and Taxpayers

A successful program also needs the acceptance and cooperation of parents and taxpayers in general. Their support and involvement will send a message to the Board of Education that a suicide prevention program is wanted, needed, and necessary.

A community task force should be set up that consists of parents, students, school personnel, and representatives from community agencies. Their input and recommendations would be invaluable and give evidence of community support. Since suicide is a community problem, it should involve the community. This task force, in cooperation with the school system, could help develop educational programs, support programs, and resource directories for the entire community.

V. ORGANIZATION OF THE SUICIDE PREVENTION PROGRAM

A. Central Office

The organization of a suicide prevention program begins at the central office and is comprised of the following steps:

1. Select and identify school support personnel. Responsibility of the central office staff will be to ensure the availability of appropriate support personnel in the schools. Support personnel could consist of school psychologist, school social worker, school nurse, and guidance counselor. Allowances should be made for specialists outside the school system to act as consultants.
2. Ensure that these support personnel are appropriately trained in the prevention, intervention, and postvention strategies of suicide. These people would implement any intervention program as well as offer support services to all teachers and students.
3. Develop a referral list of professional agencies and/or individuals who are knowledgeable and willing to work

with suicidal youths, are available as consultants, and/or will serve as a referral base.

4. Develop a general referral process. A system-wide referral process assures that one is available to all schools and allows all personnel to use the same. The process should enable a referral of a student from the classroom to any outside source if necessary.

5. Develop support materials to be used in the education or implementation of the intervention program. Such material could be films, videotapes, books, handouts, and community help sources.

6. Organize a crisis team that will be available to each and every school within the school district.

7. Ensure a program or plan of implementation for the crisis team in emergency situations and allow for practice runs before an emergency occurs.

8. The crisis team, trained in suicide awareness, would implement a program of educating teachers, staff, and students to all aspects of suicide. Issues to discuss would be the myths of suicide, the signals of suicide, classroom indicators of suicide, and confidentiality. Suggested members of the crisis team are the principal or vice principal, the school psychologist, the school counselor and/ or school social worker, and the school nurse. An outside consulting psychologist/psychiatrist is also recommended as part of the team.

9. Develop and implement a counseling process and guidelines for those students identified as high-, moderate-, or low-risk for suicide.

10. Ensure a program or plan of implementation for the crisis team in postvention situations. Postvention issues that should be addressed are the grief process and the prevention of cluster or imitation suicides.

11. Make available to the community the services of support personnel for education and awareness of suicide in children and adolescents.

12. Legal implications of the school's position in suicide prevention and intervention should be investigated as to the

school's responsibilities pertaining to the rights of the students and their families.

13. Guidelines for confidentiality should be developed in order that the rights of the students and families are protected.

B. School Implementation

After the central office has established guidelines for a suicide prevention program, it is the school's responsibility to implement the program. The following steps are suggested:

1. Organize an overall crisis plan specific to your school and the support personnel available to it.
2. Develop specific responsibilities for each team member and designate alternative duty assignments in case a team member is unavailable. Specific skills (e.g., first aid, crisis training) that may be necessary should be identified.
3. Implement an alert plan to notify all appropriate personnel in a crisis situation.
4. Educate the staff and students as to the myths and signals of suicide and the behaviors of at-risk students.
5. Educate the staff and faculty as to the referral process as it pertains to crisis situations, noncrisis situations, and "don't know what to do" situations.
6. Establish an appropriate screening process to identify at-risk students.
7. Notify the parents of those students who are at high risk, and make outside referrals.
8. Obtain parental permission and implement appropriate intervention strategies to those students who are at low to moderate risk.

Although this material does not cover all possible alternatives to a system-wide suicide prevention program, it nonetheless covers important aspects that all schools should consider. Adjustments and additions should be determined by the individual school systems.

It has not been demonstrated that suicide prevention programs are necessarily successful in preventing suicide. Nor has it been demonstrated that discussing suicide with students and faculty will cause more students to commit suicide. Garfinkel (1986) notes an unpublished study conducted by Garfinkel, Haberman, Walker, and Parsons from which "one can cautiously conclude . . . that a non-standardized educational program within a school setting directed to students and teachers is not associated with an increase in suicide attempts or severe depression in a particular high school." Research as to whether or not schools have suicide programs and whether or not there is an increase in suicide is begging the question. It is the content and approach of a program that is of consequence and needs to be examined. A program aimed at short-term intervention in suicide is probably going to be less successful than long-term programs aimed at stress reduction, problem solving, coping skills, values clarification, and the building of positive self-esteem.

CHAPTER **10**

Intervention Strategies

Because of the seriousness of the moderate- to high-risk life-threatening situation, we stress that outside help should be sought. There are often long-term problems that underlie a youth's suicide attempt and usually these problems require extensive intervention involving the family. Additionally, the time and energy necessary for this type of involvement are too much for a school setting.

For the youth who is deemed at low risk for suicide, however, intervention and involvement by the school may provide a special opportunity for learning. Nelson and Slaikeu (1984) point out that there is a striking compatibility of goals between schools and crisis services since both provide unique growth opportunities that are based on learning. Schools need to view crisis intervention as a chance to enhance coping, through improved problem solving and learning of new skills that are both cognitive and behavioral, in order to manage life's disruptions. Crisis intervention is not an added task or problem (Slaikeu, 1984).

Crisis is a temporary state of upset and disorganization. The inability to problem solve or cope with a situation results in an action that is either negative or positive (Slaikeu, 1984). The goal of any crisis intervention is to reestablish coping abilities. The person in crisis, with suicidal feelings, is or feels unable to handle circumstances that are overwhelming to him or her at that time.

In addressing crisis intervention, this chapter consists of an intervention overview, an assessment of lethality, a description of psychological first-aid techniques, first-order intervention for high-risk emergency and nonemergency crisis action, and second-order intervention techniques for moderate or low noncrisis action.

INTERVENTION OVERVIEW

Although each situation is unique and needs to be judged individually, the first rule has to be *contact the parents or guardians* even though the youth may have asked the confidant not to. Many school psychologists, counselors, social workers, and/or other school personnel worry about the confidentiality aspect of the situation. There is an underlying fear that if confidentiality is broken the student will no longer continue to confide in them. This is not true. The ambivalence, along with the rigidity of choices that a suicidal youth is experiencing, makes it imperative that someone intervene. Discuss clearly with the youth that the contact will be made so that there will be no misunderstanding on the part of the youth. When another student, teacher, or anyone expresses concern for a youth, outreach contact must be attempted. Remember—the critical factor is saving a life.

The intervention strategies discussed here will work on three levels: the affective, the behavioral, and the cognitive (Shamoo and Patros, 1985). Whereas the affective level tends to be the obvious in terms of intervention (i.e., anxiety, anger, depression, panic), all levels need to be addressed as there is a cyclic process that needs to be halted.

There is a change in the suicidal youth's behavior patterns. The behavioral level often reflects an aimless, impulsive need to react or act. There may also be a change in sleep and/or appetite patterns. An increase in tension occurs on the behavioral level. There is the feeling that something has to happen, something has to be done. Usually the youth wants it immediately, right now!

As the youth's tension increases, his or her thought processes become confused. There is an inability to concentrate, focus, or attend. A variety of cognitive errors begin to happen. As the overwhelming emotions affect cognition, thoughts become more confused, judgment is impaired, and problem-solving abilities are disrupted.

The intervention strategies will be divided into first-order intervention for both high-risk emergency and non-emergency crises, and second-order intervention for moderate- and low-risk situations. There is no single method to cope with a suicidal youth, not only because of the individuality of the youth, but also the person dealing with the youth, the situation, and the environment. The person who is involved with the adolescent or child should choose and/or individualize a particular strategy to fit the circumstances.

Whereas various intervention strategies will be reviewed, an assessment of the lethality or risk level of the situation is of the upmost importance and always needs to occur as part of the intervention strategy.

ASSESSING THE RISK OF SUICIDE

Perhaps the most crucial aspect of suicide intervention is assessing the risk level of the student who is contemplating suicide. Factors that should be considered in this risk assessment are:

1. Assessing one's intent of suicide
2. Assessing the specificity of their plan
3. Assessing the method they have available
4. Assessing the time element
5. Assessing the possibility of intervention
6. Assessing drug and/or alcohol involvement
7. Assessing past suicide attempts
8. Assessing their supportive environment
9. Assessing their anxiety/frustration level

We will discuss these factors in greater detail.

1. *Assessing one's intent of suicide.* The American Association of Suicidology suggests the following method of approaching a student suspected of having suicidal thoughts, feelings, or intent (Allen and Peck, 1977).

Begin with a statement such as "You appear to be kind of down." If the answer is affirmative, then ask the youth if he or she is feeling somewhat depressed. A yes answer would then lead to a statement such as "I guess sometimes it seems as though it's not worth it to go on struggling and fighting when so many disappointing things happen to you." From an affirmative answer, one might ask "Do you sometimes wake up in the morning wishing you were dead?" and finally with a comment such as "Have you been thinking about killing yourself?" Ease into asking about suicide in a caring and concerned way. An affirmative answer here, or even a veiled yes, should be cause for concern and continued inquiry.

In cases where there are negative responses or a hesitancy to discuss their thoughts or feelings of suicide, our approach is to move away from the topic temporarily and deal with other issues that may be more acceptable to the youth at that time. Once better rapport is established and the youth feels more comfortable, we would then broach the subject again. We would continue this process until we could make a determination of the risk level.

2. *Assessing the specificity of their plan.* A plan for suicide would suggest a high risk, especially if the plan is detailed. If the individual has indicated suicidal intent, ask questions such as "How would you kill yourself?" "Do you have a plan?" "How would you go about killing yourself?"

For example, a youth has confided to a friend that she is thinking about shooting herself and has stolen the keys to her father's gun cabinet. If intent is established, and the youth has a specific plan, risk may be high.

3. *Assessing the method they have available.* The more one has access to the method of suicide chosen, the higher

the risk. For example, if a student states that he intends to shoot himself and there are guns available to him, or if a student intends to use carbon monoxide and a car is available, then the risk is considered high.

If one has the intent, a specific plan, and the means to complete the act of suicide, then the risk is extremely high.

4. *Assessing the time element.* Time is an important factor in that if one sets a time for the suicide attempt, then risk must be considered high. If the time selected allows the student to be alone for a period of time with no expected interruptions, then completion of suicide is more possible. Since many suicide attempts by children and adolescents are after school until late night, any suggested time within this period, especially if no one will be home, is to be considered serious. For example, the youth who stole the keys to her father's gun cabinet plans to commit suicide on the weekend when her parents are away.

If one has suicide intent, a specific plan, the means to complete the act, and a time set, then the youth must be considered a serious risk.

5. *Assessing the possibility of intervention.* Children and adolescents know the expected schedule of members of the family as well as the plans of close friends. Any plan that allows for a suicide attempt when no one is expected to interrupt, or in which the method allows no intervention, is to be considered serious. There is less chance of an intervention occurring for the youth who plans to shoot herself as opposed to the youth who plans to use carbon monoxide at a time when family members may be expected home.

Any student who expresses an intent to commit suicide, has a specific plan, has the means to complete the act, and has the time set so no one can interrupt would be an extremely serious risk.

6. *Assessing drug and/or alcohol involvement.* Drugs and/or alcohol act to make a student more impulsive and reduce the youth's control over his or her own behavior. They also serve to lessen the fear of death and encourage risk taking.

Given their use by any student who is contemplating suicide, and given a number of the previous signs, then risk is to be considered extreme.

7. *Assessing past suicide attempts.* Any previous attempts at suicide should suggest that suicide is seen as one option for solving problems. What should be considered are behaviors that might be self-harming but are not viewed as a specific suicide attempt; for example, an "accidental" overdose of medication, a one-car accident, frequent overuse of alcohol and/or drugs, playing dangerous games, and so on.

With the option in place—an option we feel will persist in future years but perhaps not as a priority behavior—the risk increases when other of the previous signs are seen.

8. *Assessing their supportive environment.* Many children and adolescents who contemplate and attempt suicide feel isolated and alone. If they have few friends or cannot appreciate what friends they do have, or if they have few, if any, significant relationships with peers or adults, then there is a risk of suicide.

The more one is alone and isolated and the more other previous risk factors appear, then the more serious the risk.

9. *Assessing their anxiety/frustration level.* The higher a youth's anxiety level and the greater his or her frustration, then the more likely the youth will use desperate means to relieve it.

The risk of suicide increases when a high anxiety/frustration level is coupled with other of the previous factors. The youth who becomes unreasonably angry at minor irritations or who is easily frustrated and is quite impulsive should be carefully screened.

PSYCHOLOGICAL FIRST AID

Psychological first aid (Slaikeu, 1984) begins when a youth is in a crisis state. The purpose of psychological first aid is to reestablish immediate coping abilities as quickly as possible.

The longer the crisis state exists, the more difficult it is to intervene. Slaikeu (1984) suggests that psychological first aid is accomplished through several steps:

1. Make psychological contact
2. Clarify the precipitating event
3. Examine possible solution outcomes
4. Take concrete action
5. Establish follow-up contact and network support

Since a crisis state is fluid and unique, the steps that are presented do not need to be followed in any sequential order. It is our feeling, however, that all the psychological first-aid steps need to be introduced into the crisis situation. To be understanding to a suicidal youth is not enough. Utilizing the five steps of psychological first aid as a "map" gives structure for the adult in a situation that is tense and frightening. When a situation is not going well, the five steps can also work as an assessment tool for what is blocking the crisis resolution. An example of how the assessment might work is when the youth responds with several "Yes, but ... " comments or replies "Nothing will work." When this occurs, the adult may need to spend more time exploring the precipitating event, establishing better psychological contact, and/or examining other possible solutions again.

Make Psychological Contact

When making psychological contact with a suicidal youth, bring into the intervention situation a sense of calm confidence and competency. The hopelessness, helplessness, and haplessness that the suicidal youth is feeling requires someone who will not be overwhelmed by the youth's feelings.

To make psychological contact means to communicate concern and to encourage the youth to talk. Active listening is of the utmost importance. It establishes a psychological environment wherein a person feels free to discuss concerns and fears. There is an acceptance of what is said. Although it is not necessary to agree with the youth's view, it is necessary to understand a different perspective of the world. This means presenting no judgments.

Focus on the suicidal youth's feelings. Every message contains information and presents an emotional framework. To hear information along with the emotional tone promotes understanding. When dealing with feelings, it is not necessary to have all the answers or even to know all the questions; just be interested and concerned. Keep the suicidal youth talking; and if you don't understand something, say you don't understand. Have the youth talk and then have him or her talk more, and more after that.

Psychological contact is also made in nonverbal ways. Being physically supportive is a way of sharing the pain and upset when one does not know what to say or when there are no words that can be said. Both the youth and the helping adult should be comfortable in the manner and way of physical sharing. Examples are stroking a youth's hair, touching the youth's arm or back, or putting one's arm around the shoulder. Examples of nonintrusive support would be buying the youth a soft drink, sharing food, or taking a walk together.

Clarify the Precipitating Event

Suicide does not occur spontaneously. There is a buildup of stressors with which the youth cannot cope. Unfortunately adults tend to view the precipitating event as minor and as the only reason why the youth wants to die. The precipitating event or the crisis event is the last straw. This "straw that broke the camel's back" needs to be identified so that the felt anxiety can be controlled or at least partially reduced.

In clarifying the precipitating event, it is important that the helping adult reacts in a consistent way and avoids getting caught up in the intensity of the youth's distress. A realistic view needs to be presented and maintained for the suicidal youth. Although things may never be the same again for the youth and/or the family, a sense of hope and expectation that the youth will be able to survive the crisis should be conveyed.

There is a need to find out what has happened. What is the precipitating event, when did it happen, who is involved? This is best accomplished by having the youth tell the story.

When dealing with a youth (or anyone) in a crisis state, one finds that the strong emotion and upset that is present causes the person to be dilated and constricted all at the same time. When a youth is dilated, he or she is disorganized, confused, and vague. The listener has a hard time following the conversation, or trying to sort out who the characters are, or even what the issue is about. There are comments like "Everybody hates me," "I'm just not good enough no matter what I do," and "They don't want me around." The helping adult needs to turn the hopeless statements around to be open-ended comments; for example, "Name some people who hate you," or "Tell me what happened," or "Name someone who doesn't want you around." Asking a close-ended question will only prompt short responses, whereas open-ended comments encourage more lengthy answers. When a turnaround or open-ended statement is used, three things are accomplished.

1. An interest is conveyed. The youth is important. Someone is listening.
2. There is the introduction of alternative coping ideas. These ideas can be encouraged and explored together.
3. The youth's support network can be investigated.

Although the youth is "all over the place," he or she is also constricted. Everything is black or white. He or she is overfocusing on the problem. There are no alternatives for the suicidal person except death. This "tunnel vision" (Grollman, 1971) keeps the youth from considering any suggestions that might be given by well-meaning peers and adults.

It is important that the helping adult not be drawn into this overfocusing. What needs to be done is to define in very, very concrete terms the reality of the situation. When a youth is in a crisis state of confusion and disorganization there is an attempt to deal with everything all at once. Everything looks overwhelming and hopeless. It helps to sort issues out by time, that is, determining what has to be handled immediately and what can wait. An example of an immediate need for a youth who feels that he or she can't go home is a place to spend the night, whereas a later need might be getting a job and counseling.

Check the accuracy of the youth's perception of the problem. People's perceptions are often slanted by issues that are carried around with them. Issues can be such things as dependency, difficulty with authority, low self-esteem, and/or failure. These issues can float to the surface and contribute to a youth's breaking point. Statements that the youth makes can convey attitudes and/or self-views that will more fully identify the issues; for instance, "I failed English because the teacher had it in for me." "I failed English because I got sick and never caught up." "I failed English because I'm stupid." For a youth who is suicidal, the crisis event is the summation of all that has gone wrong in one's lifetime.

When the crisis event is identified, it helps the youth to focus her or his thoughts. When the crisis event is summarized for the suicidal youth, the message of concern is given.

Examine Possible Solution Outcomes

Involving the youth in solving his or her own problems gives the youth a feeling that he or she has some control. All too often in a crisis situation, a "helper," whether it be an adult or a peer, will rush in to offer a solution. Typically the solution will be rejected with reasons why it is unworkable. Avoid giving advice or offering solutions *until the anxiety level is reduced.* The well-meaning advice and solutions that are given too early are not going to be received by the youth and will further alienate him or her by giving the message that you don't know what's going on or that you're just like everyone else, not listening to him or her.

First have the youth relate what has already been tried,

that is, what actions the youth has taken to try to resolve the situation. Next try to have the youth come up with other solutions or different approaches to solutions already attempted. This encourages her or him to take control and dispel some of the helpless feelings that the youth is experiencing. Due to the overwhelming emotions, the adult may have to assist the youth in taking control. One method to aid the youth in coming up with solutions is by coaching him or her in a structured way; for example, "What would happen if you . . . (told your parents, called your friend, etc.)?" "Think about if you were to . . . (go to the hospital, go home tonight, etc.)." When coaching is done, the adult is able to guide the youth in fully considering previously rejected solutions or untried ideas (Slaikeu, 1984).

It is only after the youth has attempted to come up with suggestions that the adult joins in with offering alternative solutions. It is helpful to give alternatives about what to do in this particular situation, perhaps making a comment such as "What do you think about . . . (going home tonight, contacting the clinic, etc.)?" The adult then explores with the youth the pros and cons (or with a younger child the plusses and minuses) of each of the alternative solutions.

Along with exploring alternative solutions, the adult needs to aid the youth in following through with a possible solution, by realistically viewing obstacles to the plan. It is important that the obstacles be identified and worked through. Again, it should be stressed that the upset that the youth is feeling may interfere with his or her thinking, and so the adult must try to foresee any possible obstacles to a plan. When reviewing possible obstacles to a plan, it helps the youth if "practice runs" can be tried together. For example, if the youth needs to make emergency contact to a support network (either a friend, suicide hotline, or whoever) and no one is home or the lines are busy, explore what other alternatives are available aids to the youth's coping abilities. Another example would be if the youth needs shelter, talk about where and who the youth should contact.

If the upset is so great that the youth cannot participate

in exploring possible solutions, then there is a need to continue the active listening and keep the youth talking.

Take Concrete Action

The lethality of the situation directly affects whether the helper becomes the authority or a facilitator. When the assessment of lethality is high, the adult needs to take a more directive stance. This could mean anything from actively mobilizing services to taking charge of the situation. The adult may use comments such as "I am concerned for you and I may take this action . . . " or "We need to talk." Similarly, in an emergency, the adult may contact the parents and/or make arrangements for outside help for the youth. By acting directly and in an authoritative manner, the confusion, ambivalence, and rigidity of thought that the suicidal youth is displaying can be responded to.

Set the boundaries and limits by establishing rules. Be very concrete with plans. Examples of actions are to take away the pills (gun, car keys, etc.), or to make an appointment, or to drive the youth to the hospital or home.

When the lethality of the situation is deemed to be lower (i.e., no danger to self or others) and the youth is able to act on his or her own behalf, then the helper acts as a facilitator. It is the youth who is responsible for his or her actions, with the adult aiding the youth in implementing solutions.

A written contract between the helping adult and the suicidal youth can be established. (See Chapter 12 for sample contract.) This contract states that the youth will not commit or attempt suicide for a stated period of time. If the suicidal youth is feeling desperate and begins again to think of suicide, he or she agrees to make telephone contact with an appropriate adult or to a Suicide Prevention Hot Line. Remember to include the telephone numbers. Signing this contract is a concrete commitment that the suicidal youth will not attempt suicide before contacting someone. When setting a contract that a call is to be made, there is a responsibility that the adult will be available to the youth. When this is not possible, alternative sources of help (e.g., a Suicide Prevention Hot Line) should be given. These alternate sources of help need to be examined and explored with the youth. Explain how a hot line works. This explanation establishes structure and helps the youth to be less afraid. Again, it is suggested that possible obstacles be explored together and practice calls made.

Establish Follow-up Contact and Network Support

The primary focus is to check that the goals of psychological first aid have been accomplished. That is, has lethality been reduced, support given, and resource contacts established, and support network identified for the youth?

The suicidal youth may resist contact with other people, but the more contacts that the youth has, the better. Isolation is to be avoided. When a youth requests secrecy, try to explore the reasons for this request. Usually the youth is afraid of how others will react to him or her, or the youth may think that he or she is "going crazy," "cracking up." Reassure the youth that the upset, confusion, and helplessness that he or she is feeling is not a mental illness but a normal reaction to an unusual happening.

Parents or guardians need to be notified, as well as school officials. The issue of confidentiality is secondary in any suicidal behavior. Unfortunately, some parents believe that a suicide will not occur, seeing it only as an attention-seeking or manipulating behavior. Still, the contact needs to be made. No matter what the response the parents or guardians give, it is a response.

Confidential details and issues that are private to the youth and family need to be respected and not shared with "the world." However, there is a need to involve others—siblings, friends, teachers, anyone that the youth may use for support. It is important that everyone helps. Support by a meaningful network may mean the difference between coping or collapsing under pressure.

Establishment of follow-up contact should be clearly outlined. This means specifying not only a time and place, but who will call who, and if the contact will be face to face or by phone.

Prior to ending the inital contact, affirm with the youth that talking about suicidal feelings and thoughts was the right thing to do. Do this very concretely; for example, "I'm glad you told me. It was the right thing to do." This will erase any feelings of guilt and embarrassment that the youth might be feeling.

If the youth is suicidal and is unable to control self-destructive impulses, then hospitalization may be necessary and may be the most logical course of action that can be taken. Also, if the parents or guardians are unresponsive or uncooperative, then contact to the state's protective services for children should be made.

FIRST-ORDER INTERVENTION

HIGH-RISK CRISIS

Emergency: A Suicide Has Been Attempted

In a suicide attempt, immediate action is imperative for the physical survival of the youth. The essential features in a high-risk emergency situation are:

1. *Physical survival and safety of the youth and others*
The first priority is always the safety of the youth and others. Emergency first aid may be necessary. Emergency calls should be made (i.e., calls to the parents or guardians and, if needed, for an ambulance and/or police).

2. *Determination of method* Among the actions to be undertaken is determining the method. For a drug overdose, the drug or type of drug, amount of drug taken, approximate time of ingestion, and the youth's weight are important information. For a method higher in lethality, such as firearms, knives, and so on, immediate notification to the police is es-

sential. The safety of others, as well as that of the suicidal youth, are primary issues.

3. *Notification* If parental contact cannot be made, the school should have intact a policy to initiate emergency room or hospitalization procedures. If parents or guardians are not cooperative, then the state's protective services should be notified.

4. *Documentation* After the crisis situation, documentation of events by all involved should be made. This documentation, made by the team leader or an administrator, should contain events and contacts prior to the suicide attempt, actions taken by staff, persons notified, and outside referral contacts. Postvention plans should then be initiated.

5. *Follow-up* Although the school is not actively involved in therapy where there has been an attempted suicide, continued contact and communication with the suicidal youth is suggested under the auspices of the private therapist. It is felt that the more support network that the youth has available and the more concern and caring expressed for the youth's welfare, the better. Follow-up contact for a suicidal youth eases his or her embarrassment and aids the transition back to school.

CASE HISTORY
AN EMERGENCY HIGH-RISK CRISIS

Mary is a fourteen-year-old freshman. She is an only child whose parents were divorced approximately three years ago. Mary's mother was concerned that her daughter was depressed or angry over the divorce. Until a few months prior to the visit, the mother described her daughter as being overly good, always trying to say and do the right thing. At the time of the referral, Mary had begun some acting-out behavior—drinking, smoking pot, and having sexual relations. She was cutting classes and failing all subjects. Mary presented herself as remorseful, commenting, "I fell in with the wrong crowd at school, and I will never do any of that again"; all she wanted was to have "my mother's trust again."

Mary was in therapy for approximately six months before her suicide attempt. During this time Mary kept the facade of "everything's perfect, I'm trying to win my mother's trust back." Behavior began to deteriorate, however. Mary's asthma medication began to disappear at an alarming rate, due to her continued pot smoking. Cut notices from the school were sent and intercepted by Mary before her mother could see them.

Mary made her suicide attempt in the school psychologist's office by swallowing a collection of medications. The school psychologist was busy with another student and did not realize that Mary was unconscious in the outer office until the other student had left.

The school's emergency crisis plan was put into immediate effect. An ambulance was called, as was the poison center, which was given the names of the medications ingested, Mary's weight, and an approximate guess as to time taken. Mary's mother was notified at work and informed that Mary was being taken to the local emergency room and that she should go directly there. The school psychologist accompanied Mary in the ambulance to the hospital and stayed with her and her mother until Mary was out of danger. In discussing the suicide attempt briefly with Mary, it was found that Mary's friend, Debbie, had given her the pills.

The Superintendent of Schools was notified by the principal, as were members of the crisis team, to alert them to Mary's suicidal attempt.

Outreach to Mary's close friends was made. This proved to be an important step since Mary's best friend, Debbie, had given her some of the pills, and knew that Mary was thinking about killing herself. Debbie was filled with guilt and confusion over her part in Mary's attempt, although Mary had made Debbie promise not to tell anyone. Reaction to Debbie's part by other friends of Mary's was very hostile. These students were excused from the rest of the day's classes and were sent to the school social worker who set up a group to discuss the attempted suicide. After the group meeting, Debbie's parents were notified of the events of the day and requested to come to the school to take Debbie home.

Documentation of the day's events by the principal began almost immediately. Teachers who expressed concern and/or asked questions about Mary were simply told that she had ingested some pills and had been hospitalized.

The day after the suicide attempt, Mary was visited by the school psychologist at the hospital. Friends and teachers sent get-well cards. This outpouring of feelings encouraged Mary and laid to rest for her some feelings of "What will they (friends) think about me?"

After Mary's hospital stay, therapy continued with her private therapist. The school continued to be involved with Mary, acting as a support network between Mary, her mother, and the private therapist.

Nonemergency: A Suicide Is Viewed as Immediate and Life-Threatening

A youth who is at a high risk for suicide means that lethality is high and/or there is an inability to cope or act on his or her own behalf. Once it has been determined that a youth is at high risk for a suicide attempt, the intervention has five parameters.

1. *Suicide reduction* Make contact and form an alliance with the suicidal youth as quickly as possible. This is accomplished by following the psychological first-aid techniques that were outlined in the previous section. Again, it is stressed that although the sequence of the steps is not important, *all* the psychological first-aid steps need to be utilized. (See Chapter 12 for a sample suicide contract.)

2. *Implementation of safety and "watch" guidelines* If the youth is in possession of the means to commit suicide, attempt to have the youth surrender it. Unless it is a weapon, make the request to the youth that you want the means of suicide so that you can better help him or her. Have someone with the youth at all times; do not leave him or her alone. If a weapon is involved, do not hesitate to ask for security/police aid. Commonsense should prevail, keeping in mind your own safety and the safety of others.

3. *Parental and "official" contacts* Parents or guardians should be notified and requested to come to the school for a

conference and to pick up the youth. It should be clear that the parents or guardians *must* come to the school. At the conference the seriousness of the situation and the school's concerns should be discussed and documented. If parents or guardians are not cooperative, then contact the state's protective services.

4. *Referral*   A referral list of professional agencies or individuals who are knowledgeable and willing to work with a suicidal youth should be given to the student and to the parents. Parents should be requested to sign a release form so that the school may share pertinent information with the consulting agency. Request that the parents or guardians call and notify the school of the actions that they have taken and in whose care the child has been placed. If the parents do not call, then the school should call for the necessary information. If a parent or guardian refuses either to respond to the school's concerns or to arrange for the safety of the youth, then the school should notify the appropriate social service agency and/or the police.

5. *Documentation*   Documentation of the school's concerns is necessary. Following the parent conference, a letter reviewing the parent/school conference as well as a statement regarding the school's concern for the youth's welfare and well-being should be sent to the parents, with a copy placed in the youth's confidential file.

6. *Follow-up*   Follow-up contact with the youth should be established to monitor progress. If the youth is hospitalized, contact with the youth should ideally be made during his or her stay and definitely prior to release. This is done to keep rapport with the youth, to facilitate the transition back into the school environment, and to encourage follow-up therapy on an outpatient or private basis. Upon the youth's return to school, an appointment or an outreach contact should be made by the appropriate school personnel to keep the lines of communication open.

Hopefully, arrangements for follow-up therapy will be

made on a private outpatient basis. The school should view its services as supportive only, and should not attempt therapy with the high-risk student due to the volatile and serious nature of the situation.

CASE HISTORY
A NONEMERGENCY
HIGH-RISK CRISIS

Betty is a fifteen-year-old high school sophomore. Her mother abandoned her and her older sister when Betty was ten months of age. Her stepmother of twelve years is the only mother that she has ever known or can remember. There are no other siblings except her older sister.

Betty presented herself at the school social worker's office and requested a "cut pass." When questioned about why the cut pass was needed, Betty became extremely agitated and angry. The social worker began the psychological first-aid process and soon discovered that Betty thought she was pregnant by her best friend's twenty-year-old boyfriend, who was the local drug dealer. An assessment of lethality determined that Betty (1) did have a suicide plan (carbon monoxide poisoning); (2) did have the means available (her mother's car); (3) knew where the spare car keys were kept; (4) had a set time (after school before her mother got home from work; approximately three hours); and (5) knew her sister had after-school activities that would delay her arrival home.

During the course of the interview, Betty revealed that she had made a previous suicide attempt some months ago, cutting her wrist with a razor blade after carving a boy's initials into her arm. At that time, her older sister had stopped Betty's attempt. Betty's feelings were that she really was going to kill herself, and that she was going to make sure that no one was around this time.

Betty was kept in the office with the school social worker while appropriate contacts and actions were undertaken. Betty's parents were immediately contacted and requested to come to school. At the parent conference, it was decided that Betty should be hospitalized immediately. Her overwhelming despair and depression were obvious, and she steadfastly maintained that no one could stop her from killing herself. She stated, "My family has to sleep sometime; they can't watch me twenty-four hours a day."

The parents transported and admitted Betty to the local hospital's psychiatric ward. A permission form had been signed at the parent conference so that the school social worker could talk to the hospital's therapist.

Documentation of the parent conference, along with a report by the social worker of the circumstances and events leading to the crisis situation, were made within twenty-four hours. This was sent to the parents and a copy was placed in Betty's confidential file.

After Betty's dismissal from the hospital, the school social worker had an appointment with her on her first day back to school. Since Betty and her family were involved in out-patient therapy at the hospital, it was felt that only supportive contact by the school's social worker would be maintained.

SECOND-ORDER INTERVENTION

MODERATE RISK

A Suicide Is a Possibility and Is Being Considered

A youth who is at a moderate risk for suicide is the most difficult to correctly assess. Usually this youth has the desire to die, but does not have the means nor has made a concrete plan for execution. Some support network is available and a total breakdown in coping is not yet experienced. Intervention takes the following form:

1. *Establish a rapport* Follow the psychological first-aid guidelines discussed in the previous section. The youth needs to know that someone is concerned about his or her well being, that someone is listening, understands, and accepting. This initial contact provides an opportunity for the adult helper to ascertain how the youth asks for help, the youth's strengths and weaknessess, and the support network that is available to the youth. Listen for facts (what happened?) and feelings (how did the youth react to the event(s)?). By recognizing the anger, depression, and anxiety, the helper reduces

the emotional intensity and begins to redirect energy into problem solving.

2. *Request a "No-Suicide Contract"* Request that the youth sign a "No-Suicide Contract." (See Chapter 12 for a sample contract. Also see Take Concrete Action under the Psychological First Aid section.) Briefly this means that the youth agrees not to kill himself or herself while in contact with you. Under this contract, the youth also agrees to contact immediately the appropriate personnel or a "crisis hot line" if there is a feeling that he or she cannot adhere to the contract. If the youth refuses to sign the contract, this automatically places the youth at a higher risk level. (See High Risk, earlier in this chapter.)

3. *Limits of confidentiality* Explain to the youth that confidentiality does not exist for suicide or homicide. Parents or guardians will be notified.

4. *Parent appointment* Arrange for a parent conference as quickly as possible, hopefully within twenty-four hours. At this conference, documentation of the school's concerns should be made, a referral list of agencies or individuals who work with suicidal youths should be given to the parents, a release of information form should be signed so that pertinent information may be shared with the consulting agency or individual, and a request should be made that the parents, the consultant, and the school all work together to aid the youth.

If the parents or guardians are not responsive to the needs and safety of the youth, contact the state's protective services for children.

5. *Documentation of the school's concern* A follow-up letter to the parents or guardians outlining the events and issues discussed during the conference, as well as an expression of the school's concern for the youth's well-being and welfare should be sent as soon as possible. A copy of the letter should be placed in the youth's confidential file.

6. *Time-out*   Permit the youth to have a "time-out" haven during the school day if it is needed. Offer to have the student return to the "helper's" office at any time during the day. When this is not possible, arrange for the youth to have an alternate place to go when feelings become too overwhelming.

7. *Appointment with the youth*   An appointment should be made with the youth. If the appointment is not kept, then outreach must be attempted.

8. *Alert*   Appropriate school personnel should be alerted to the possibility of suicidal intent. The school should be cognizant of the family and youth's need for privacy and should operate under the "need to know" policy. Details that were given in confidence by the parents and/or youth should not be discussed except when permission is given and only to specified individuals. If the youth increases visits to the health room, appropriate personnel need to be informed. Increased frequency could signify a movement toward a higher level of risk.

CASE HISTORY
A MODERATE RISK

Jeff is a seventeen-year-old honor roll high school student. He participates in various extracurricular activities and is well liked by teachers and peers. Jeff had expected to attend an Ivy League university but recent family financial difficulties has now made that unlikely, unless he wins a substantial scholarship. In an attempt to help his family, Jeff took a part-time job after school but this has caused his grades to drop dramatically. His parents have recently separated and Jeff's mother has a serious heart condition.

Jeff's girlfriend of two years has just recently asked that they be "just friends" so that she can date other people. In order to "prove" his friendship, Jeff gave his ex-girlfriend all of his record collection and old pictures of the two of them together.

Because he was concerned about Jeff, a favorite teacher tried to spend some time talking to him about future plans.

Jeff's responses were so unlike him that the teacher decided to take his vague concerns to the school psychologist.

The school psychologist initiated contact with Jeff. Concern was expressed about all the hard things that have been going on in Jeff's life. Although encouraged to talk, Jeff's conversation was stilted and he was obviously ill at ease. It was only when he was asked if he had ever thought about killing himself that Jeff began to talk. He had been thinking of killing himself but was concerned about how this would affect his mother's health. Although he did not have a definite plan, he did have a time picked out. His mother was going out of state to visit her sister and Jeff felt that that would be an "ideal time" as there "would be someone with her when she got the news."

His giving away of the records and pictures was his way of saying "good-bye" to his girlfriend and sparing his mother the "trouble of clearing out my junk."

Jeff was asked to sign a no-suicide contract with the school psychologist. Although he thought it was "silly," Jeff did sign the contract. A crisis hot line number, as well as the school psychologist's home number, was given to Jeff. A strong recommendation was made for him to see a psychologist outside the school for counseling. A referral list was given to him and the school psychologist told Jeff a little bit about each one of the people on the list. Jeff's parents were contacted, and a parent conference was arranged for the next day. Jeff's parents did not keep their appointment with the school. Contact with the parents only elicited vague excuses. A letter expressing the school's concerns along with a referral list was mailed to the parents. A duplicate copy was placed in Jeff's file. It was later that week that Jeff's father shot himself in the family garage. His mother found her husband and immediately collapsed. Jeff took charge of everything—the funeral arrangements, visits and consultations with the doctors, the police and the lawyers.

Aware of the events in Jeff's life, the crisis team met and, in their discussion, it was decided Jeff was a high-risk student. An alert to Jeff's teachers was sent so that any clues or concerns could be immediately brought to the crisis team's attention.

Approximately a week after his father's funeral and a day before his mother was to be released from the hospital, Jeff phoned the school psychologist for help. Jeff felt that life was not worth living, his mother was going to die soon (his perception), and there was no one at all to love him or be concerned about him. Life was "just a dead end."

An assessment of lethality was made, and the psychological first-aid process begun. Jeff, at the end of an extended conversation, decided that he would "give it another week," and would definitely see the school psychologist first thing the next morning.

For the next week Jeff continued to keep in contact with the school psychologist. It was during this period of time that Jeff asked the psychologist to help him set up an appointment for therapy.

Jeff continued to use the school psychologist as a source of support while he was in therapy.

LOW RISK

A Suicide Has Been Thought of but No Plans Made and No Action Taken

In this case the youth has vague feelings of not wanting to go on, and is feeling helpless and hopeless. There are no plans for suicide and no explicit threats have been made. However, there is the possibility that the youth could escalate to a moderate or high risk. This youth has the greatest possibility to benefit from primary intervention. The following intervention steps are suggested. (Guidelines for steps 1 through 5 have already been reviewed under Moderate Risk.)

1. Express concern.

2. Request a "No-Suicide Contract" from the student.

3. Give the youth a twenty-four-hour emergency phone number.

4. Arrange a parent conference.

5. Alert appropriate school personnel of concerns.

6. In order to keep contact with a low-risk student, arrange brief "as needed" visits with the youth and/or a weekly short status report from teachers.

7. The possibility of short-term counseling should be considered and investigated, as it is this type of youth that would benefit the most from a primary intervention at the school level. Aiding the youth in learning to solve problems and to cope are tasks that are well suited for the school environment. (See Chapter 12.)

CASE HISTORY
A LOW RISK

Stacy is a ten-year-old, learning-disabled fourth grader. Her parents have been having marital difficulties and have separated several times in the past; as Stacy says, "They are getting re-vorced again." Stacy's overall appearance is one of dishevelment and neglect. She has stolen, is not liked by her classmates, and is constantly being picked on by them. Teachers report that Stacy is "clingy and whiney." Lately, Stacy has started masturbating in the classroom.

It was for the latter behavior that Stacy was referred to the pupil personnel team. Contact was made by the school social worker. Visits to the school social worker were scheduled for a short-term needs assessment. It was during one of the visits that Stacy spoke of her sadness, and how "everything was messed up and couldn't ever get better." Stacy felt that her grandmother, who had died the year before, "had it lucky cus she don't have to worry no more." Stacy talked of how she wished she could "be up in heaven too."

At the Pupil Placement Team meeting, with parents' approval, Stacy continued her visits with the social worker for short-term counseling and also became part of a group that was working on behavioral changes and social skill building.

To summarize, we have discussed in this chapter how to assess lethality, explained the psychological first-aid process, and identified and described the actions needed in the various risk levels. However, in order for the process to become an active, integrated part of the school's environment, preparation and practice are necessary components.

As a final comment to this chapter, an evaluation of the

process should always be done after an intervention has occurred.

All case studies are a composite of actual cases changed to insure the confidentiality of the students and their families.

Do's and Don't's of Suicide

Do	Don't
Do take all threats seriously.	Don't ignore or explain away suicidal comments.
Do notice signs of depression and withdrawal.	Don't explain away sudden behavior changes.
Do be concerned if there is a loss of a loved one, even a pet, or a loss of self-esteem.	Don't think that a youth will get over it.
Do trust your own judgment.	Don't be misled.
Do tell others.	Don't keep a confidence for fear that you might be overreacting or look silly.
Do express your concerns to the youth.	Don't sermonize, moralize, or use guilt tactics.
Do stay with the youth if there is a crisis.	Don't assume that the youth will be all right alone.
Do, if safety permits, remove the means of suicide.	Don't leave the means of suicide available to the youth.
Do notify parents of your concerns.	Don't use vague language. Be specific with your concerns.
Do refer to a professional.	Don't handle it yourself.
Do stay in touch with the youth.	Don't assume that just because a referral was made that the youth won't need your support.

Do's and Don't's in the Assessment Interview

Do assess lethality and do psychological first aid.	Don't let one's fears minimize the situation. Don't ignore danger signs.
Do try to appear calm.	Don't panic.
Do listen carefully.	Don't tell your story. Don't make judgments.
Do ask questions.	Don't assume anything.
Do try to keep the person to concrete facts.	Don't get caught up and pulled into the youth's emotional turmoil and confusion.
Do establish a timeline (which issue needs immediate attention; which issue can wait).	Don't try to solve all issues at one time.
Do take responsibility.	Don't assume that somebody else will handle it.
Do explore possible obstacles to action.	Don't ignore possible problem areas that would hamper or discourage the youth from coping.
Do establish follow-up contact.	Don't assume that there will be follow through on the referral or intervention plan.
Do consult with other professionals.	Don't handle it alone.

CHAPTER 11

Postvention

By virtue of being an institution of learning, the school is in a unique position to teach children about life and death. Not to do so is an avoidance of its responsibility. Suicide is one of the factors in life that needs to be addressed since it is a frightening and often incomprehensible act. However, in any postvention program, focus should not be mainly on the suicide but on the behaviors which led to the feelings of hopelessness, helplessness, and depression. It is important to emphasize other methods of dealing with one's problems and feelings and to discuss the idea that there are sources of help through the school and/or the community. Emphasis should be on seeking help as a strength, not as weakness, and that we all can and do have problems that may, at times, benefit from intervention.

The days and weeks following a suicide are difficult and stressful. Thus, a postvention plan should be developed well before a crisis. Focus should be mainly on the students but certainly with concern for faculty and staff also. The overwhelming emotion that spreads throughout the student body must be addressed. There is surely a great deal of confused feelings, anxiety, fear, and even guilt.

An initial approach should be to deal with the suicide

in an open and honest manner. Students must be given the opportunity to discuss openly their thoughts and feelings. Since children (as well as adults) find suicide a difficult topic to discuss, the school must take the initiative that will allow for open discussion. Students and faculty must be given accurate, verified information about the suicide, and information about suicide in general, covering the negative social, emotional, and psychological behaviors leading to suicide. The purpose of stressing social, emotional, and psychological dysfunctioning is to discourage identification with the suicide and thus hopefully to discourage subsequent suicides. Areas that may be probed and discussed in relation to the suicide at hand are problems the youth may have been having in school, at home, with his or her peer group, physical problems, alcohol/drug-related problems, and acting-out behavior. Seen from this perspective, it may discourage students from identifying with the suicide. It also allows school personnel to focus on stressors and not the suicide itself (Garfinkel, 1986).

The major thrust in any discussion or information giving is that most problems can be adequately resolved and that seeking help is a desirable strength. Sources of this help should be detailed.

Death, especially a suicide, shakes the very foundation of a youth's being. For the child, death is confusing and frightening. For the adolescent, who views the self as indestructible, the death of a peer challenges his or her coping resiliency. For the adult, a youth's suicide leaves one ill-prepared to handle one's own felt fears and inadequacies.

What to do after a suicide is of major importance if emotional traumas, crippling scars, and cluster or imitation suicides are to be avoided. As tragic as a suicide is, it becomes even worse if the effects on students are not tempered by adequate intervention by significant adults. School personnel, as significant adults in the lives of children and adolescents, are in a position to be positive factors in postvention strategies.

The following steps, listed in priority, should be undertaken by appropriate personnel following the suicide of a student. The timing of each step is best left to the individual school since circumstances will vary.

THE PRINCIPAL

1. Upon learning of a suicide, the principal must ensure that he or she has accurate information regarding all aspects of the suicide. He or she should endeavor to speak with someone of authority who has first-hand knowledge of the suicide. Communication should have been made with police/authorities long before any tragedy, and some policy should have been established regarding such information.

Information that may be helpful is the time of death, the method used, the location where the suicide took place, and any reason for the suicide that may have been determined. It may also be helpful to contact all of the special services within the school to see if that child was receiving their services and for what reasons. This may afford the principal a clearer profile of that youth and the stresses that the youth was experiencing.

2. Notify the crisis team and meet with them to set up the timing and implementation of the postvention program.

3. Immediately notify all faculty and staff, and set up a meeting for the earliest time possible to ensure that all personnel have the same accurate information and to lend each other support. Since most suicides occur after school, it may be necessary to telephone all teachers and staff directly or through a telephone fan-out system. If the suicide occurred after the school day, schedule a faculty meeting for the morning of the next school day. If the suicide took place during the school day, schedule the meeting immediately after school. The crisis team should attend this meeting.

4. Inform the student body of the suicide. This may be done in one of two ways. Probably the best approach would be for the teacher, along with a crisis team member, to discuss the facts as he or she knows them from the faculty meeting. The crisis team member can be there as support for the teacher

while also observing students who may have a strong reaction and also need support.

In large schools, there will probably not be enough crisis team members to couple with each teacher. It may then be best to assign crisis team members to those classes formerly attended by the suicide victim, or classes where he or she was best known.

Some schools may wish to consider notifying the students by way of the public address system, after giving the teachers the same information in a faculty meeting. The teachers could then offer the students support, and crisis team members could be assigned to the classes normally attended by the suicide victim.

5. Allow for and plan an adjusted class schedule, if necessary, to enable teachers and students an opportunity to discuss the suicide and to express their thoughts and feelings.

6. Have substitute teachers available throughout the day for those teachers who need or require a "time out" period while adjusting to or dealing with their own reactions toward the suicide.

7. Arrange for the consulting team specialist to be available at the school for a reasonable period of time. This is to lend support, give information, and act as a consultant to the intervention team.

8. Announce the wake and/or funeral arrangements. Faculty and staff should be encouraged to attend, appropriate to the school schedule and their relationship to the suicide victim.

9. Be in contact with the public as necessary. All material intended for the public and media should be disseminated through the principal.

10. Arrange for a memorial service in school to commemorate the child's life, not his or her death. The death should be treated no differently than any other, nor should it be prolonged or made special.

11. Arrange an evening meeting, perhaps in conjunction with the PTA/PTO, open to the community to discuss suicide in children and adolescents and to review steps taken in the school to support the student population.

12. Coordinate all aspects of the postvention process.

13. Express support to the family. Someone designated by the school should be available to the family as a contact person. That person may help the family with any school-related matters that may need attention (e.g., returning books, cleaning out lockers, and so on).

THE CRISIS TEAM

1. Meet with the principal prior to the faculty meeting to lend support, coordinate known information about the suicide, and set the timing and implementation of the postvention program.

2. Be available at the school for faculty and student support as well as for faculty meetings. The team should be responsible for ascertaining, as much as possible, what behaviors, feelings, and attitudes were exhibited in the days, weeks, perhaps months prior to the suicide. A comprehensive profile would help all faculty and staff see the suicide in perspective. Care should be taken to protect the rights of the student and his or her family. If the student was being seen at the school for special services, care should be taken not to violate any confidentiality that may exist.

3. Attend the faculty and staff meeting to lend support and to answer questions regarding the suicide and/or suicide in general.

4. During the faculty and staff meeting, discuss the methods and techniques for helping students express their thoughts and feelings. Orient teachers as to what types of reactions to expect from children at various age levels.

Behaviors that may be seen by teachers and parents in

children and adolescents who are not dealing appropriately with the death are:

a. Fear of returning to school, as evidenced by increased absences and truancy by adolescents, and unexpected and inappropriate classroom behaviors in children

b. Clinging to parents (i.e., not wanting to separate or being overly concerned about where the parents are)

c. Somatic complaints; increased visits to the health room

d. Won't go out to recess

e. Won't participate in extracurricular activities

f. Isolating oneself by shutting out external stimuli by utilizing music, fantasy (i.e., Walkmans, stereos, boom boxes)

g. Increased peer group activity and outside home and school involvement.

5. Set up a crisis center at a convenient and appropriate location where students and school personnel can be seen for individual help and support.

6. Be aware of and offer support to especially close friends, as well as enemies, of the suicide victim. Due to possible feelings of guilt and responsibility that may be attached to the suicide, these students may be especially vulnerable and in need of outreach.

7. For those classes in which the suicidal student was enrolled, a member of the crisis team should meet with the class to discuss:

a. The accurate information known by school personnel about the suicide.

b. The thoughts and feelings of the students regarding the immediate suicide and suicide in general.

c. The actual suicide, in order to put it into perspective (i.e., it was the individual's choice—not something forced onto him or her by fellow students, relatives, friends, or enemies). Briefly discuss reasons why children and adolescents commit suicide, emphasizing the negative psychological, social, and emotional elements, thus discouraging students from identifying with the suicide.

    d. Myths of suicide and any rumors that may have started.

    e. Any fears or anxiety the students may feel about themselves, friends, or relatives.

    f. The fears and/or misconceptions of death in general.

    g. The availability of special personnel at the crisis center to offer individual help and support.

  8. Be available to any class or grade, as necessary or desired, to discuss the same factors listed in #7 above.

  9. Meet with peer counselors (if such a program is available at the school). Peer counselors are given the same accurate information as faculty and staff, and are allowed an opportunity to react to their own thoughts and feelings. Discuss information regarding suicide and make suggestions for how to deal with their peers. Any students for whom peer counselors feel concern should be brought to or encouraged to go to the crisis center. Concerns for these students should be discussed with the crisis team members. For those students with known concerns, outreach by crisis team members should be initiated.

10. Assess the suicide risk level of students referred to the crisis center or of students for whom teachers and peers have expressed concern.

11. With parental notification and permission, refer high-risk students to the consultant psychologist or psychiatrist. If permission is not given, contact should be made with the state's child protective service.

12. Contact parents of students who were unusually affected by the suicide to offer support and assistance in dealing with their child. In extreme cases, it may be suggested that the child be taken home, provided there is a parent home to render support.

13. With parental permission, make arrangements for short-

term individual and/or group counseling for students who require additional support.

14. Be available to talk with concerned parents, faculty and staff, and members of the community regarding suicide. Special attention should be given to teachers who taught the suicide victim, as they may feel some responsibility or guilt (i.e., they may have given the student a failing grade, or reported some infraction of the rules, or felt that they "should have seen it coming").

15. With parental permission, as an aid in preventing future suicides, do a psychological autopsy of the suicide. This psychological autopsy, consisting of known feelings, attitudes, and behaviors prior to the suicide, should be presented to the faculty and staff for their growth and development.

16. Maintain an ongoing liaison with the principal and consultants.

17. Have appropriate and reliable sources of referral available for students and faculty and staff who need outside professional help.

18. After the team has been activated and the emergency is over, meet to evaluate the team process and to make any necessary changes.

Care should be taken by crisis team members to protect the rights of the student and his or her family. If the student was being seen at the school or outside the school for special services, care should be taken not to violate any confidentiality that may exist.

THE FACULTY AND STAFF

Custodians, secretaries, aides, clerks, nurses, and other personnel are as important to the postvention process as the teachers and administrators.

1. Attend the faculty and staff meeting called as soon as possible after the suicide.

2. Allow for the sharing of feelings, emotions, and support with other faculty and staff. The expression of feelings allows for the reflection of fears and anxieties and makes one better able to handle the events in the classroom and school.

3. Participate in the planning of an approach to dealing with the thoughts and feelings of the suicide that are appropriate for specific students and grade levels. Ask special services personnel for assistance.

4. Encourage children in the classroom to discuss the suicide and to express their thoughts and feelings. It must be stressed that suicide is not a heroic act; thoughts of this type must be discouraged.

5. For classes in which the victim was enrolled, allow for involvement in the grief process. This may be done by writing letters, making sympathy cards, creating a bulletin board display, and so forth.

6. Inform students as to the availability of special personnel at the crisis center and the location of the center.

7. Students for whom teachers or staff are concerned regarding their response to the suicide should be brought to or encouraged to go to the crisis center. Follow-up contact should be made with the crisis center by the teacher or staff member to be sure students were seen or are known by the team.

8. Faculty and staff who might have been especially close to the suicide victim should seek individual help and support from the crisis team.

9. Ask for free time, if needed, to provide opportunity to come to terms with the suicide.

10. Allow for the expression of support to the family of the victim.

11. Be available to students and parents for information and support. Official information should be through the principal.

12. Attend the faculty and staff meeting after the first school day to discuss the events of the day and to discuss and share concerns. Plans should also be made at this meeting for any follow-up classroom activity deemed necessary. Allowance is made for faculty and staff to express their thoughts and feelings.

Care should be taken by faculty and staff to protect the rights of the student and his or her family. If the student was being seen at the school or outside the school for special services, care should be taken not to violate any confidentiality that may exist.

THE PSYCHOLOGICAL/PSYCHIATRIC SUICIDE SPECIALIST

This consultant should have training and experience in suicide, suicide prevention, and dealing with the aftermath of suicide.

1. Be available at faculty and staff meetings for support, information, and suggestions.

2. Be available to individual students and faculty and staff for support and to assess their emotional status and suicide risk.

3. Be available to meet with parents as a group to discuss their thoughts, feelings, and concerns regarding suicide.

4. Be available to the crisis team and principal for additional support and/or relief, and for consultation.

Care should be taken to protect the rights of the student and his or her family and to safeguard confidentiality.

CHAPTER **12**

General Intervention Strategies

Due to the increasing number of children and adolescents with depressed and suicidal behaviors coming to the attention of school personnel, this chapter will suggest some examples of specific intervention strategies. Remember that it is the health and welfare of the youth that is *always* the paramount issue for any decision concerning intervention and/or short-term counseling. For some youths, problems are too involved, too intense, and too volatile to be handled within the school system, in which case referrals to an outside mental health agency or other professional should be made. However, if it is determined that the needs of a youth can be addressed within the school setting, then the approaches presented in this chapter may be helpful.

Determining which youth to serve within the school setting and which youth to refer out is not always clear. This is a judgment call. For the youth who is deemed a low risk (see Chapter 10), early intervention could be effective. However, if at any time the person who is working with a particular youth is unsure or has an uneasy feeling, then refer out. It cannot be stressed strongly enough the seriousness of working with a depressed and/or suicidal youth.

This chapter is divided into three parts. Part I presents a

sample of an interview with a depressed and possible suicidal youth, a sample anti-suicide contract, referral and follow-up contact issues, guidelines for conducting a parental interview, and confidentiality issues.

Part II is written for teachers or those who have contact with children and adolescents but who are not mental health professionals. Suggestions for stress management techniques, self-esteem enhancement within the classroom, social skill development, and problem-solving techniques are presented. These will not only aid in the prevention of depression and suicide, but will also assist children who feel good about themselves in more effectively dealing with their stresses.

Part III is written for the mental health professional who is familiar with counseling techniques and is qualified to do short-term counseling with low-risk youths. A brief overview of the various therapy theories will be presented, with general therapy goals outlined, followed by issues to be addressed, and specific therapy exercises for elementary and secondary grade levels.

For anyone to reach any youth effectively, it is beneficial to utilize a variety of the youth's sensory modalities (i.e., the youth's tactile sense, verbal skills, and listening skills). Connecting feelings to a physical action helps many children and adolescents to learn to identify issues. Recognizing a feeling or issue is the first step toward learning how to cope. We believe that just as it is beneficial to utilize all of a youth's sensory modalities, utilization of all of the school's resources could make a difference in reaching a youth.

PART I

Prevention of suicide is an ongoing process that needs to be continuously reviewed and updated. All to often, after a crisis situation has been successfully acted upon, there is a lessening of responsibility and a let-down period that occurs. Focusing attention on a youth who is suicidal may stop an action now, but if help is not obtained, and the suicide act or thought is denied by significant people in that youth's life, what will happen to that child six months, nine months, or even years later? It is our belief that suicide will remain a viable option in that youth's repertoire of coping strategies.

INTERVIEW WITH A DEPRESSED AND/OR SUICIDAL YOUTH

The following interview is an example of an initial contact with a student who may be depressed and/or possibly suicidal. It is not meant to be used verbatim, but should be adapted to the situation and to the particular youth.

Comment
When talking to a troubled child or adolescent, ask questions that reflect concern and are supportive. Remember always to take the time to build a rapport with the youth. The message that the interviewer wants to give is one of an understanding and supportive attitude. To skip this first step may reaffirm the youth's fears that he or she is worthless and helpless. Omitting this first step can also create frustration for the interviewer.

Sample Interview

Jim is a seventeen-year-old junior. He is on the football team, but has been cutting classes and practice lately. Both his coach and teachers report a mood change. One of Jim's friends has spoken to the school psychologist about Jim, expressing concern that "he's becoming more and more out of it."

At first, Jim is silent and obviously uncomfortable.

Comment
Body language communicates messages for both parties. The message the interviewer wants to give Jim is, "I am listening to you. You are important." Therefore, the interviewer listens attentively, not only to Jim's words but his pauses and intonation.

I: "Jim, thank you for coming by to see me. I guess you must feel a little strange coming in to see the shrink."

J: "Yeah, I don't know why the coach sent me here. Everything's OK."

I: "Well, he's noticed that you've been down lately and he thought perhaps I could help."

J: "He's always thinking somebody's down. Just because you get into a slump, he thinks it's some big deal. I don't need to be here. Everything's OK."

Comment

When dealing with a youth who is noncommunicative and/or uncomfortable, it is sometimes helpful to ask about a happier or less stressful time and then identify those feelings to encourage talk.

I: "I remember how well you played last year and you started off pretty good this year."

J: "I had it together then."

I: "And you don't now?"

J: "Umm . . . No . . . There's just a lot of stuff happening now. . . ."

I: "Oh, like what sort of stuff?"

J: "School, practice—I haven't been playing too good lately. Maybe I am in a slump. Coach said my concentration's off. Must be right—I can't keep my mind on anything. I just got too much stuff on me. I'm on overload."

I: "You're right. Sounds as if you are getting overloaded, too much going on. Maybe we can sort some of this stuff out?"

Comment

The interviewer should not interpret to the youth how the youth *really* feels or *should* feel, but rather be accepting of what has been said. The trust has to be built and will grow as the interviewer listens.

J: "That will be the day. There's way too much junk in my life. No one can sort it out. What good does it do to sort out garbage? No one cares for garbage. I don't care. Just garbage. My whole stinking life's garbage."

I: "With all those feelings, it must be impossible to hold all the pain in. It must seem that life's not worth living when you feel this way?"

J: Silence. "Well it's not."

Comment

When the youth is able to be angry and let other emotions out, then the trust building has progressed. The interviewer acknowledges those feelings of being angry, overwhelmed, afraid, or hopeless.

I: "Do you ever wake up in the morning and wish that you hadn't? That you were dead and out of this stuff?"

J: "Yeah, well, it's not worth it. I know what you're going to ask next, shrink, you're going to ask me if I'm going to kill myself . . . Uh?"

I: "I guess you do know what I'm going to ask next. Have you thought about killing yourself?"

J: "Sure. Who hasn't? OK, so I've been thinking about it. Now you're going to call my folks, tell the coach, tell the teachers, tell the world. Tell everybody that I'm crazy."

Comment

It is necessary to call the youth's parents or guardians. It is also important to know the youth's support network (who are his friends? etc.). The youth should be assured that he or she is not crazy and that it was smart to reach out for help.

I: "No Jim, you aren't crazy. However, I do have to let your parents know how you are feeling. I'm glad that you let me know how you feel, I want to help you. Is there anyone else that you can share these feelings with?"

Oftentimes in an interview the youth will first deny any feelings or thoughts about suicide. When this happens one should return to the task of building a rapport. Talk and focus on other issues or subjects, then bring the direction back to how the youth is feeling. For instance, "Gee, it sounds like you're pretty down (or blue). It also sounds as if things are pretty rough for you right now. It must be so hard for you to keep on going. Have you ever thought about killing yourself?" If the youth again denies any thoughts of suicide, accept the statement but focus on how you would like to help. Keep the communication lines open.

The assessment interview for lethality is presented again in this chapter so as to provide a cohesive view of the entire interview process.

In the lethality interview process, it is important to ascertain the following information:

1. Is the youth planning to kill himself or herself?

"Have you ever thought about hurting yourself?"
"Do you ever feel so down or blue that you wish you were dead?"
"Do you wish you were dead?"

Returning to the sample interview, Jim has been thinking of killing himself.

2. Has the youth made a previous attempt at suicide?

"Did you ever try to kill or hurt yourself before?"
"Have you ever felt this way before?"
"What happened when you felt this way?"

For example:
I: "Jim, have you ever felt this way before?"
J: "Yeah, about two years ago. My girl and I had a fight.

Really thought I'd drive my car into a tree. Only reason I didn't is that we got back together."

3. Does the youth have a plan?

"How would you kill yourself?"
"If you have thought about hurting yourself, do you know how you would do it?"

For example:
I: "You feel like killing yourself now. Have you thought how you'd do it?"
J: "The same way. I've got my car."

4. Are the means to kill oneself available to the youth?

"Do you have gun?"
"Do you know where or how to get a gun?"
"Do your parents or friends have a gun (or pills, etc.)?"

For example:
I: "Do you have your car now?"
J: "Yeah."

5. What is the youth's time frame? (If the youth is specific about when he or she plans to kill oneself, then the risk is higher.)

"When will you do this?"
"Have you thought about when would be a good time to kill yourself?"

For example:
I: "Jim, when are you planning to take your car and run it into a tree?"
J: "I don't know. Sometime. I just got to get the nerve up to do it."

6. Does the youth have access to alcohol and/or drugs? (If yes, then the risk is increased because there is less self-control and because impulsivity and false courage are increased.)

"Have you taken any drugs or have you been drinking?"
"How much have you had to drink?"
"What have you taken?"

For example:
I: "How would you get your nerve up?"
J: "Umm, probably I'd load a few beers on. Helps me forget this garbage."

7. Is there any chance of rescuing the youth? (The more isolated the setting, the less chance there is for discovery and rescue.)

"Whose around?"
"What time will someone get home?"
"Where is this place?"

For example:
I: "This tree, is it the one out on Mountain Road where it curves around on the way to school?"
J: "Yeah, that one."

8. Who is the youth's support network? (The more isolated the youth feels, the greater the risk.)

"Who else can you talk to besides me?"
"Where are your parents (guardians, friends)?"
"Who can you share these feelings with?"

For example:
I: "I know that Tom's your best friend. Do you talk to him too?"

J: "All the time. He knows everything."

I: "He sounds like a good friend. Someone who wants to help too."

What has been presented is a condensed version of the interview process. In Jim's case, he and the interviewer wrote up an anti-suicide contract, Jim's parents were notified, and an outside referral for professional help was made. Contact by the school psychologist with Jim was made throughout the school year.

For further clarification, Glaser's (1965) classifications of warnings for youths who attempt or complete suicide are given here.

Just talk   This is a casual expression stated by the youth and is viewed as common. However, remarks that are frequently repeated should be followed up with further evaluation.

Expressions such as "I wish I were dead," "I want to disappear off the face of the earth," and so on can be casual statements without any thought of suicide behind them. However, if the statements are given frequently and if the youth's mood and behavior pattern has changed, then there should be further evaluation.

Gesture   A self-destructive or harmful behavior has occurred that is planned to draw attention to the youth.

This can be seen in a teenage girl who has superficial scratches or cuts on her wrists, or in a boy who has carved initials into his arm. Unfortunately, many people see these gestures only as a way to get attention and not as a way to get attention to stop a suicide.

Threat   A threat is hard to distinguish from "just talk" and is more serious than the "gesture." Usually there is a history of unresolved stress, with feelings of inadequacy and of being overwhelmed.

The teenager who feels there is "no hope" and that "no one can help" is at higher risk than the teenager who engages in a self-destructive act. This is because there is the possibility that conflicts are deeper and unresolved.

Attempt   The most desperate of all warnings, there is a definite risk present.

The youth who has a plan and the means for suicide, but leaves a note indicating what he or she is planning to do and where he or she is, is making an attempt at suicide but is hoping for rescue. Unfortunately, for many who make an attempt, their plans for rescue may not happen.

ANTI-SUICIDE CONTRACT

The following is an example of an anti-suicide contract. Whether a contract is signed or not signed, parents/guardians should be notified of the potential for suicide. Review with the youth what the contract means and its importance once it is signed. Sometimes in order to have a youth sign an anti-suicide contract it is necessary to have repeated follow-up contacts or comments, with the message of "I care and I don't want you to die, I don't want you to do this," along with repeating a specific plan of action (e.g., plan to see the therapist the next day, contact a physician, talk to parents, etc.) (Hatton and Valente, 1984).

The goal of the anti-suicide contract is to buy time. There is a need to reduce the lethality of the situation and remove any weapons that might be available. Slaikeu (1984) suggests that the ambivalent feelings that have emerged in the discussion be utilized in forming and personalizing the suicide contract. An example of this would be if the youth states "I want to die, but I don't want my mother to be hurt," then suggest postponing the suicide decision for a few days because of the youth's love for his mother and an unwillingness to hurt her. The purpose of the anti-suicide contract is to have the youth cooperate in not committing suicide for an agreed period of time.

ANTI-SUICIDE CONTRACT

I, _____, promise not to kill myself
until I talk to you first by phone or in person. I promise
not to do anything that is harmful to myself, intentionally
or unintentionally, by virtue of some of my behaviors (specify what behaviors are of concern, for example, drinking,
drug use, etc.) for the next_____(specify
the time limit).

Have the youth read the contract aloud. Do not let him
or her mumble or garble the words. The words must be said
aloud, clearly, and without any doubt of the meaning, with
the time limit of the agreement stated specifically. Do not
permit the youth to shrug his or her shoulders or say vague
"um-hms." Whereas it is permissible for the youth to say the
contract in his or her own words, the meaning and time
limits must be clear and specific (Hatton and Valente, 1984).

If the youth refuses to sign, this is an indication that
safety procedures must be carried out. Emergency calls and
contacts should be initiated with or without parental approval. If parental approval is not possible due to the emergency of the situation or inaccessibility, then immediate and
appropriate action must be taken. This action may mean hospitalization or police contact.

An example of a recent intervention occurred in our office when a young client brought her friend to see her
"shrink." A highly distraught, pregnant fifteen-year-old girl
had just been dumped by her boyfriend. Parents had thrown
her out of the house when the pregnancy became known and
were refusing all contact with her. The girl was at a high
emergency risk level as she had a suicide plan and the means.
She refused to sign the anti-suicide contract or to stay in the
office. The therapist contacted the parents but was unable to
involve them or elicit any concern. Due to the high risk and
the refusal of the parents to become involved or to take responsibility, the therapist contacted the police and the state
department of children's services. In the assessment interview, the therapist had been able to obtain names and tele-

phone numbers of friends. This information was given to the authorities. The girl was located and placed in protective care.

If a youth is unwilling to promise to take precautions against suicide, then there is a need for more direct involvement. If high lethality is not reduced through psychological first aid or by an anti-suicide contract, then hospitalization may be the only safe option available. Contacting parents/guardians is the first step. If at all possible, make this contact with the suicidal youth present since open and honest communication is essential throughout all of the intervention. For example, state to the youth that there is concern for his or her safety. "Tom, I'm worried about you and I don't think that you should be by yourself tonight. Either you can call your parents or, if it would be easier for you, I will." If parents/guardians are unavailable or not responsive, then contact with the state's protective service should be made.

If the youth is of legal age, voluntary hospitalization should be suggested. This can be presented to the youth as a "time-out" period—a time where no decisions have to be made. Reassure the youth that he or she is not crazy. For example: "It sounds as if too many things are happening to you right now. Everything's coming down all at once. Why not take a 'time-out'? I'm suggesting a stay in the hospital to give you some breathing space. You're not crazy, you just need time to help yourself get some control."

If the youth is at high risk for suicide and is not cooperative, then involuntary hospitalization is necessary. The involuntary hospitalization should take place under the guidelines of local law.

Remember, as the level of lethality increases, intervention becomes more directive so as to ensure the safety of the youth.

REFERRAL NEEDS

For the depressed and/or suicidal youth who is at high to moderate risk, discuss with him or her the need for professional help outside the school setting. The youth will need ongoing therapy that the school will not be able to provide, and involving the youth in planning for this will improve chances of a successful referral.

1. Explain to the individual why a referral is necessary. Stress that the youth is not crazy, but needs help in sorting out stressors in his or her life.

2. Review briefly with the youth not only those events that precipitated the crisis and brought about those feelings of being out of control, but also areas of concern that need to be addressed in a therapy setting.

3. Involvement of parents/guardians and significant others to support the referral aids the process. Utilize the youth's support network as much as is feasible, while still being aware of legal and confidential standpoints. A youth in crisis fears what peers will say to and/or about him or her. Often peers will shoot down the referral and even talk the youth out of ongoing contact.

4. Tell the youth as concretely as possible what to expect. If referral is made to a private therapist whom the facilitator knows, sharing that or other bits of information is beneficial. If the referral is made to a mental health facility, discuss what the youth should expect. For example, some mental health facilities do an intake interview then make the therapist/client assignment. Other situations that may arise are that the therapist may want to see the entire family, the youth alone, or a combination. If a suicide or a hot-line phone number is given to the youth, role-play or model for the youth what occurs when the call is made.

5. Try to anticipate obstacles or resistances to the referral. These obstacles may be due to the youth's own inability to take action or due to denial by the parents/guardians that there is a problem. Will transportation and/or therapy costs be problems? Will a letter be needed for the school or anyone else to secure time off? Who in the school should be notified

that the youth is a moderate to high risk and will be involved in therapy? Will the youth become scared and back off from further involvement by deciding that he or she was overreacting or being silly?

6. If the youth is of legal age, obtain a signed release of information.

7. Explain to the youth why follow-up contact is necessary. Express your concern to the youth that you want him or her to live and be better able to cope with life's stressors.

8. Most importantly, affirm to the youth that he or she made the right decision to share thoughts and feelings. Make this affirmation very concretely; for example, "I'm glad that you told me how you feel."

For the youth who is at low risk for suicide, and counseling intervention is to be within the school environment, explain as concretely as possible the reasons for counseling, identifying the issues and goals that will be worked on. Also review with the youth the areas of confidentiality. Be honest with the youth about what you will need or be required to share with parents/guardians or authorities.

FOLLOW-UP CONTACT

A successful strategy in preventing suicide is follow-up contact by a designated person to determine if an outside referral has been acted upon. This simple tactic is often overlooked or forgotten, particularly when an initial stress situation is felt to be resolved.

For those students who are at a high to moderate risk for suicide, it is important that not only an outside referral be made for further evaluation and determination of need for ongoing treatment, but contact with a designated person be maintained. This should be done in conjunction with parents, the private therapist, and, of course, the youth. Too often, after a referral has been made there is a lessening of concern on the school's part.

If a youth has been absent from school for some time, contact with the student should be made upon his or her reentry to the school. The person to make the contact should be determined prior to the youth's return. Usually the person who had initial contact with the youth serves as the contact person. Since this is not always feasible due to time restraints, scheduling difficulties, and so on, another person can be selected. Regardless of how the contact person is selected, the rapport with that youth should be a prime factor.

The purpose of the contact is to convey to the youth the concern and caring of the school, to ease any embarrassment or awkwardness that the youth may be feeling, and to establish or perhaps reestablish a support network.

PARENTAL INTERVIEW

When conducting an interview with parents/guardians, the school's concern as to the seriousness of the situation has to be conveyed, and in such a way as to be accepting to parents/ guardians who may not wish to hear the message either because it is too scary or there are guilt feelings. In many cases the parents/guardians have had the feeling "that all was not right" but were unsure of what they were seeing, hearing, or feeling. The confirmation by the school will give them the direction and impetus to seek help.

It is important to let the parents/guardians react and talk. In a sense, there is a need to employ the psychological first-aid techniques that were discussed in Chapter 10. In effect, the message of suicide is creating a crisis within the parents/ guardians. When there is denial, there is a need to project blame onto an external source or to intellectualize the behaviors away. For those parents/guardians who react with denial, for whatever reason, utilize active listening and then state and restate as concretely as possible the school's concerns.

Often parents/guardians view suicide as a way to get attention, a foolish prank, an accident, or a punishment to them. What needs to be stressed is the felt hurt and confusion that the youth is feeling. All too often, the youth is able to convey these suicidal feelings in an interview with a caring, sensitive person, but will either exaggerate or minimize these feelings when with parents/guardians.

In the interview, first state the school's concern and the felt seriousness of the situation. Use the word *suicide.* Permit the parents/guardians to react, deny, rationalize, or express whatever feelings may surface. Utilize active listening. Restate the school's concerns, emphasizing clearly and concretely the level of risk or possibility of suicide. Have available a list of mental health professionals or agencies that deal with depressed and/or suicidal youths. Discuss with the parents/guardians the professionals and agencies on the list, supplying any information that you have concerning various ones. This could be simply where a professional is located, or that previous referrals have been made to a particular person before, or information on payment fees, or so on.

Obtain a signed release of information. The school will need permission to talk to the therapist so that pertinent information might be shared.

Let the parents/guardians know that documentation of the school's concern will be made. It should be stated that personal family details are not included in this documentation. What is included is the felt level of suicide risk, the school's concerns regarding the youth, that intervention has been recommended, and that parents/guardians agree or disagree to therapy or seeking outside help. Always have another school person present at the parent conference. Do not, however, load the meeting with extra people. This is too overwhelming for parents and is not necessary. Be cognizant of the nature and sensitivity of the meeting.

Establishing an alliance with the family results in continued support for the youth within the school, the obtaining of pertinent information about the youth's ongoing life within the school and home, and modification of those aspects of the youth's world that may fuel the depressed state.

CONFIDENTIALITY

Confidentiality is a central issue. Many facilitators, educators, and peers of the youth are confused as to when to keep or break a confidence. Whenever there is concern for the life of a person, then the confidence should be broken. The principal duty is saving a life, not creating a relationship between you and the youth.

Discuss with the youth during the initial conference that confidentiality is not an absolute and that there are limitations. Clearly indicate that if the youth is thinking of suicide or of hurting another person, then appropriate contacts will be made.

Peers should be encouraged to break the conspiracy of silence and take responsible actions for suicidal friends. A suicidal youth will often choose a peer with whom to confide his or her thoughts. In a survey of 120 high school students as to whom they would tell if they ever considered suicide, 91% chose "friend" (Ross, 1985).

Confusion over whether "to turn a friend in" stems from youths' desires to be independent versus dependent (a mentality of "us against them") and conflicting friendship loyalties (wanting to help a friend by telling someone but fearful of losing that sacred trust of friendship because they did tell and broke a secret). Unfortunately, in most school systems there are no clear guidelines for youths of what to do if a friend is suicidal. Educating children and adolescents about suicide is essential if there is to be a stop to the rising statistics.

Educators are often faced with a similar dilemma. "Do I tell and break the confidence? She will never trust me again?" "Suppose I'm overreacting? Will I look like an alarmist?" "What if I put the thought of suicide in his head?" Much of the confusion for educators is a lack of knowledge regarding the referral process, determining risks and confidential limits. Educating the educators is the first step in the prevention process.

Fear of contagion is often cited as a reason for keeping talk of suicide secret. This only fuels the mystery and confuses issues relating to confidentiality.

There is an ethical, if not legal, duty to warn others if there is an imminent danger either to the youth or to others. The recent decision by the California Supreme Court in *Tarasoff* v. *Regents of the University of California* (Knapp and Vandesreek, 1982) mandates that whenever there is a danger to another person or to the actual client, then the therapist must release information. Other court rulings appear to be mixed; therefore, the facilitators need to be familiar with the laws of their particular state.

PART II

It is our premise that early contact can make a difference for those children and adolescents who are at risk for depression and have suicidal ideation. We are not suggesting that teachers do therapy. What we are suggesting are techniques that can be used within the classroom to reduce stress, build better self-esteem, and help youngsters develop better coping skills. School personnel have an unique opportunity to know and reach a troubled youth.

STRESS MANAGEMENT TECHNIQUES

Chapter 6 dealt with stress in teachers and students and presented suggestions for reducing stress. We now discuss suggestions for specific approaches for use within a classroom.

Stress is an extra demand made upon our bodies that exceeds our resources. It is a common feature of our life, experienced by everyone at one time or another. A youth's fears and anxieties are just as stress provoking as those of adults. Unfortunately, children and adolescents do not always recognize stress or know how to deal with it. Some react to stress by getting headaches or stomach problems, or experiencing mood swings and short attention spans. Others may react to stress by striking out, being sarcastic, or talking back. What is occurring is a mental distancing from the situation because there is no feeling of control and no hope of learning how to control the event.

There are two influences that we have on stress. The first is the ability to learn to control events in the environment. The second is the ability to look ahead. Unfortunately, many depressed and suicidal students have never learned how to handle their environment nor do they have the resources or life experiences that enable them to look ahead. Stress education and management within the classroom can aid all youths in developing the ability to respond to a stressful situation in a positive and constructive manner.

Nurturing Classroom Environment

Encourage students to accept a challenge and take some risks, explaining that mistakes are made to learn from, not to create shame or guilt. Recognizing when stress is working for or against a student is difficult. New tasks arouse anxiety in many children. Speaking in front of the class or going to the blackboard can be stressful for some. Structuring a situation or a new activity can turn the event into a positive learning experience. Let's take, for example, a child who is stressed when he has to go to the blackboard. Give the child a problem you know he can solve, let a friend go to the board with the child, and have the stressed child quietly whisper to the friend how the problem was solved. When stress is present and the student is able to confront the situation instead of avoiding it, that is one step toward learning to control the environment.

Stress Education

Dr. Antoinette Saunders, a child psychologist who runs a stress clinic for children, offers the following approaches for helping children and adolescents learn to identify stress and how to handle it (Reed, 1984).

A stress journal   Encourage students to keep a journal about their feelings and to draw pictures of how stress looks to them and how it affects them.

Role-playing   Encourage students to act out a typical stress situation within their daily lives, whether the stress is at home or in the school.

Turning negative statements into positive ones   Teach children and adolescents to say things positively instead of in a negative manner.

Relaxation

There are several relaxation methods available. Most of the techniques used with children and adolescents have been derived from adult exercises. Whereas the end goal of doing the relaxation exercises is the same for children and adolescents as it is for adults (that is, a reduction of stress), the main difference is that the techniques are presented more as a game experience.

Dr. Saunders presents a quick exercise called "Quick Relax" or "Breathing Feet" to help young people relax. Simple, effective, and short, the technique consists of four steps and takes about six minutes (Reed, 1984).

1. Know when you are upset or scared. Remember, everyone feels that way some time.
2. Smile inside and say to yourself "I can be quiet."
3. Breathe slowly. Imagine you have air holes in the bottom of your feet. Think how it feels to have the cool air come up your legs, to your stomach, to your head. Hold that air for a second, then let all the stressful air go out.
4. Think of the cool air coming in and the stressful air going out. Think of someplace that you like to be where you are happy and relaxed.

Humphrey and Humphrey (1985) also offer several ways to teach children and adolescents to relax.

Progressive relaxation The youth is taught to compare the difference between tensing and relaxing one set of muscles after another. Humphrey and Humphrey (1985) teach children and adolescents progressive relaxation by playing a game of "Mirrors." In their method, the adult faces the youth (or group) and asks the youth to "mirror" what the adult does. Another way to teach progressive relaxation is by playing "Simon Says." Students must do only what is prefaced by the words *Simon Says.*

Creative movements In this method, the youth or group creates their own body movements. The purpose is to tense either the entire body or a specific muscle group (such as the arms, legs, etc.) then to relax them. As an example of how to start the activity, Humphrey and Humphrey (1985) suggest that the leader ask "What is the difference between a jump rope and a bat?" The leader then suggests that the children make their arms stiff like a bat (hold for approximately six seconds), then states "Now quick, make your arms like a jump rope." Questions can then be asked of the children, such as "How did your arms feel when you made them like a bat? A jump rope?"

Another technique is to have children tense their muscles and pretend that they are wooden soldiers or robots, then quickly relax their muscles and feel like a rag doll.

Imagery In this technique the leader encourages the child or adolescent to picture the scene that the leader describes. In our work with children and adolescents, we use key words such as *warm* and *soft,* and a specific color. "Think of being curled up in a warm place. A place that has yellow sunlight. A place that is quiet. A place that feels soft under your body. A place where you can close your eyes and feel how the warm sun feels. It makes you want to stretch in the warm, yellow sunlight. Stretch your arms over your head. Feel the warm, yellow sunlight on your arms. . . ."

Meditation It is our experience that meditation works best if the child is over ten years of age. Basically the technique is the same as for adults. There is a need for a quiet place where there are no interruptions. The youth should be encouraged to get into a comfortable position. Have the youth pick a word or phrase or even hum a sound. The youth is then encouraged to concentrate and listen to how his or her breath goes in and out as he or she says the word or phrase.

There are several good resources available for reducing stress. Some examples are *Controlling Stress in Children* by Humphrey and Humphrey (1985), *The Relaxation Response* by Benson (1975), and *Helping People Change: A Textbook of Methods* by Kanfer and Goldstein (1975).

SELF-ESTEEM TECHNIQUES

Children and adolescents need a sense of self that is positive and honest. There is a need for a realistic perception of one's strengths and weaknesses, to be sensitive to the complexities of emotional expression of themselves and others, along with a need for children and adolescents to be aware of the feelings of others.

Positive Praise and Reinforcement

A simple but very effective technique to reduce stress and raise self-esteem is to praise children and adolescents. Knowing that something was handled well and receiving recognition for such is important. Unfortunately, this technique is often overlooked in a busy classroom or in a hectic schedule.

Games

In their book *100 Ways to Enhance Self-Concept in the Classroom,* Canfield and Wells (1976) do indeed offer over one hundred ways for educators to enhance a youth's sense of identity and self-esteem. Some of their suggested exercises are Adjective Wardrobe, Nicknames, Making It Real, and Car Wash.

Adjective Wardrobe The students have eight pieces of paper. On each paper they write an adjective that describes them. They then rank order the adjectives, placing the one they like best on top, the least on the bottom. They now have a wardrobe of words they can keep or discard. They are to look at each word and decide if they want to wear it or discard it. They are asked to fantasize about what kind of person they would be without that particular quality. How would they feel? They then try on that word again. Now how do they feel?

Nicknames The class discusses names that would make them feel good, proud, or self-confident. What names would make them feel bad? The class then talks about nicknames that they have been called in the past and how they felt with those names.

Making It Real The students decide what they feel to be their greatest strength as a person. They then pick the one word that best describes it. Then the students move around the classroom like the words they have chosen. The whole body is to be that word. They are to exaggerate their positions. They then stop where they are and think of the opposite of their word. Thinking of that new word, they move around the room and act out that word. The students are then asked to become their original word again. At the end of the exercise the students talk about how they felt with those feelings. Canfield and Wells developed this from an exercise by Janet Lederman (1973).

Car Wash In this activity the students stand in two parallel lines, close together. One student is sent through the car wash (that is, between the two lines) and everyone touches him or her and gives praise, affection, and encouragement.

The exercises that we have shared are condensed versions, and we recommend Canfield and Wells's book *100 Ways to Enhance Self-Concept in the Classroom* (1976) for further ideas and suggestions.

PROBLEM-SOLVING TECHNIQUES

Self-confidence and positive self-esteem are fostered by understanding how to approach and solve problems. Children should be taught how to analyze a situation and to determine what to do. The successes and failures in responding to different situations will give them the experiences they need to then choose more successful actions. They learn that appropriate action is better than no action, or indecision, or worry. They also learn that not being successful is better than not trying at all.

Children and adolescents are encouraged to try out an alternative technique that they feel comfortable with, with the understanding that it may take time for that alternative to be successful. Suicidal and depressed youths often have problem-solving difficulty, thus finding more success in this area will help them develop greater self-esteem.

What if . . .

A "what if" approach is usually acceptable by most children. They are asked what they would do under various circumstances, such as "What would you do if you were being teased by another student?" They will give various responses and the teacher/counselor can give other possibilities (Schaefer and Millman, 1981).

Examples of "What if . . ." questions that we have used are:

"What if . . . the class leader is always putting you down?"
"What if . . . someone says something bad about you and everyone believes it?"
"What if . . . you are at a party and everyone ignores you?"
"What if . . . you are taking a test and your best friend, who couldn't study last night, wants to see your answers?"

Self-Questioning

This approach, suggested by Bask and Camp (1986), applies basically to cognitive problems, but can be used in the classroom. Children can be taught to consider four questions:

1. "What is my problem?" helps them focus on the specific problem.
2. "How can I do it?" helps them consider various alternatives in dealing with the problem.
3. "Am I using my plan?" helps them focus on their predetermined approach and helps them stay on task.
4. "How did I do?" helps them evaluate the results of their action so that problems of a similar nature can be more successfully addressed.

Task Breakdown

Some youths are easily overwhelmed when given a difficult or different type assignment. Many are so disorganzied that they are unable to structure themselves. As an aid, teach the youths to break the problem down into small parts.

1. "What do I already know about this?"
2. "What else do I need to know?"
3. "Where can I find it?"

This relieves the pressure that the child or adolescent has to know everything all at once (Johns and Johns, 1983).

Alternative Solutions

Another strategy in problem solving that helps one to reduce stress and learn to cope is to encourage youths to look at a problem in more than one way. An example that is quickly and easily used is to have the youth or group brainstorm how to get over a tall brick wall, or how to get off a deserted island. Youths learn that there are different ways to look at and solve a problem.

SOCIAL SKILLS TECHNIQUES

Children and adolescents who have an impoverished social network due to poor social skills are more vulnerable to social isolation and possible depression. By improving a youth's social skills, he or she gains social recognition, which aids in improving self-confidence and self-esteem.

In general, social skills are defined by Cartledge and Milburn (1986, p. 7) as "socially acceptable learned behaviors that enable the person to interact with others in ways that elicit positive responses and assist in avoiding negative responses from them." Social behaviors should be taught and encouraged in the classroom.

In suggesting the teaching of social skills, Cartledge and Milburn (1986) summarize the selecting of social skills as follows: An identification of what skills are important to the child should be made. It is necessary to keep in mind several factors that could affect the learning, retention, and utilization of the social skills. These factors are the child's cognitive and developmental levels, the culture and situation, as well as the perceptions of those in the child's environment who will value, react to, and do the reinforcing.

Selection of those social skills that are problem behaviors for the child could be drawn from interviews with the parents, from peers, by various social skill inventories, or by classroom observations.

All too often children are so caught up in their own thoughts and anxieties, especially depressed children and adolescents, that they are not attending to what is being said or, more importantly, they are not tuned in to the nonverbal signals. Therefore, often the first step in teaching children social skills is to teach them how to listen.

Second, show children how to make friends. This can be accomplished by showing a child how to greet another child, how to ask for and receive information, and how to offer or ask to be included in an activity.

Third, the child may need to learn how to give and receive positive interactions. Modeling how to talk silently to oneself and asking questions about how to proceed are effective techniques and can easily be demonstrated.

Games

Cartledge and Milburn's book *Teaching Social Skills to Children* (1986) has a variety of ideas and exercises for social skill building. Examples of cooperative games for fun are given in a chapter by Mara Sapon-Shevin. The purposes of these games are to (1) include the child who has been isolated, (2) share with others, (3) help other children, and (4) talk nicely to other children. Some of the suggested games are Frozen Bean Bag, Hot or Cold, Touch Blue, and Ha-Ha.

Frozen Bean Bag Each child in the class moves around the room while balancing a bean bag on his or her head. The leader changes the action by asking the others to go faster, or skip, or hop, and so on. If a beanbag drops off a child's head, then that child is frozen. To be unfrozen, another child has to retrieve that child's beanbag and place it back on that child's head without dropping his or her own (Orlick, 1978).

Hot or Cold Hide an object while one child is out of the room. The child then tries to find the object. Other children call out "Hot" or "Cold" as the child approaches or get farther away from the object (Arnold, 1972).

Touch Blue One child announces "Everyone touch blue" (or whatever color or object the child chooses). Each child then touches that color or object on another child. Variations are endless; for example, "Touch an ear with a right elbow" (Harrison, 1976).

Ha-Ha This exercise requires a lot of floor space. Each child lies down and puts his or her head on the stomach of the child next to him or her. The first child in line says "Ha," the second child says "Ha-Ha," the third child says "Ha-Ha-Ha," and so on down the line, always increasing the number of "Ha"s by one (Harrison, 1976).

PART III

The mental health professional who elects to do short-term counseling with a youth deemed to be a low risk for suicide should proceed with extreme caution. If at any time there is an acceleration to a higher level of risk, then referral to an outside agency or other professional is imperative. Another consideration is that there is often too short of a time period to work effectively within the school. It is more harmful to a youth to begin counseling only to terminate because the school year is completed. Therefore, think carefully before initiating counseling.

A youth at low risk for depression and/or suicide is a child or adolescent who may have low self-esteem, poor coping skills, an inadequate support network, a history of chronic stress, with thoughts about dying. In conducting an interview with such a youth, recent research suggests that a youth may either exaggerate or minimize suicidal expressions to his or her family, but will be less distorting of his or her symptoms in an interview alone with a mental health professional. The youth's reports of her or his degree of rage or unhappiness appears to be a reliable predictor of suicide (Gispert et al., 1987; Robbins and Alessi, 1985).

When undertaking therapy with a depressed youth, the cognitive development level should always be taken into account. A youth's ability to cope in various situations and when confronted with differing kinds of stress or problems may vary with his or her degree of development. Intervention may need to focus on one particular area according to the child's specific development level (i.e., strengthening social skills, improving self-esteem, self-reinforcement training, learning problem-solving skills, etc.).

The following suggested approaches are not intended to be all-inclusive but are simply examples of approaches that can be utilized. The basic intervention strategies revolve around social skills training, behavior modification (behavior therapy), cognitive therapy, peer counseling, and group counseling. Anyone trained in a counseling format should be able to expand on any process. They are all intended for use with children and adolescents who are depressed and/or with suicidal ideation. They can certainly be used with problem behavior in general.

SOCIAL SKILLS TRAINING

Because so many of the youths that we see are lacking in appropriate social skills, training in this area is sometimes the first step in therapy. When a youth is depressed, there is often an inability to deal effectively with the social environment. The goal of this type of therapy is to teach or enhance social skills so that positive reinforcement is received. Remember, it is necessary to clarify if the youths have the social skills but are not using them from those who do not have the skills intact. Therefore, behavior observations are important prior to any therapy.

Skills that could be taught, if needed, include such specifics as voice quality, eye contact, posture, and global qualities such as making friends, relating and helping others, controlling anger, being assertive, and increasing social behavior. Various methods are discussed.

Instruction

Talk with the child about those qualities that other children have that would make him or her socially successful or not liked by others. Qualities of socially successful youths could be children who are helpful to others, pay attention to what one is saying, are concerned about someone, are friendly, are able to see another's point of view, are tuned in to body language, and give approval to others.

Goal Setting

Outline with the youth his or her areas of difficulty. Try to obtain at least five social situations that the youth wants to work on and then rank order them going from the easiest to the hardest. Examples are talking to someone on the playground, asking to join a game, asking for help, or sharing a treat.

Modeling

Modeling is when there are behavior changes that are the result of observation (Bandura, 1969). When a person is depressed, anxious, and under stress he or she is not alert to incidental cues in his or her environment. There is a misreading or even a blankness in the perception of the cues that prohibits or lessens the effectiveness of using modeling as a therapy technique. However, we have found that if a youth can be helped to focus on important incidental cues, then utilization of modeling can be a therapy avenue. It is best if the model is approximately the same age of the youth and the same sex. After the youth has talked about the desired behavior, and perhaps has observed such behavior in his or her peers with the counselor (the counselor may need to point out the behavior), then the youth is ready to role-play the behavior.

Rehearsal

Practice is more effective and efficient if the youth has an idea of what may or may not happen. Role-playing with the therapist is an important part of social skill training. One of the mistakes that is commonly made is that role-playing is discontinued too early. Usually the therapist mistakenly believes that the youth has incorporated the material more quickly than is the case. That is, the therapist, who has a higher skill level, assumes that the youth is comfortable with that skill. After role-playing the specific behavior, with attempts to anticipate all possible variations, the youth is ready to try the behavior with others and in new situations.

Feedback

Before the real-life trial, review the behavior and the goal with the youth. He or she then tries the specific behavior. Be careful to monitor for the youth how and where the behavior is to be tried. Don't let him or her try the new behavior in a difficult situation. The new behavior needs to be tried in the least problematic situation with the fewest negative consequences. At the next session, after the real-life practice, the therapist reviews how the child or adolescent did. What kind of responses did the youth receive from others and how did those responses make him or her feel?

Homework Practice

We often have a youth do social skills homework. The youth thinks and writes out imagined social situations. Encourage him or her to remember the purpose of the situation, or what he or she wishes to obtain from the social interaction.

Situation Logs

Ask the child or adolescent to note in a log those social situations that he or she sees and perhaps would like to participate in. These "real situations" are talked about and role-played between the youth and the therapist.

For increasing activity level, it is assumed that the youth has the required skill but is not producing it and that anxiety is not inhibiting the skill. If anxiety is the underlying problem, then it is the anxiety level that needs to be addressed (Kaslow and Rehm, 1983). In talking with the youth and/or parents it is usually found that the youth has in the past engaged in the behavior and it has been enjoyable. There is now a withdrawal from that behavior. To increase the activity level, review with the youth other enjoyable behaviors and possible intrinsic and extrinsic rewards. Utilizing a variation of the Premack principle, there is a pairing of an enjoyable behavior with the behavior from which the youth has withdrawn.

BEHAVIOR MODIFICATION (BEHAVIOR THERAPY)

For children and adolescents who are anxious and under a great deal of stress, we have found that behavior modification techniques are effective in some cases. Behavior modification is an approach where desired behaviors are encouraged and reinforced while undesirable behaviors are discouraged with elimination of those behaviors as a goal. The main emphasis for this approach is the reinforcement of desired behaviors which may, in some cases, constitute control by the adult. However, since control is not an unusual part of a child's environment, it becomes a matter of how much control and how it is used.

There are three major elements to be addressed for the depressed and/or low-risk suicidal youth when utilizing a behavior modification approach.

1. The contribution that the youth makes to his or her own distress by continuing self-defeating behaviors
2. The youth's perception of how much he or she can control events
3. An inability to look into the future positively

Ringness (1975) presents the following principles:

1. In most instances, we are trying both to reduce inappropriate behavior and to institute desirable behavior.
2. The inappropriate behavior to be reduced is carefully observed for frequency and the conditions under which it occurs.
3. One tries to see what is reinforcing the undesirable behavior.
4. One tries to determine more appropriate behavioral objectives. Those objectives are discussed with the youth and he or she is encouraged to accept them as alternatives.
5. The contingencies are stated.
6. One then consistently reinforces the youth for his or her appropriate behavior.
7. Posttreatment data are gathered at intervals to see how the treatment is working. If it is not working, perhaps the reinforcers or some modification of the technique should be tried.

Use of praise, rewards, contracts, and token economies, many of which are self-administered, are various ways that a social worker, school psychologist, or counselor can help teachers enhance a child's self-esteem and reduce stress.

Behavior modification techniques can be used with children, keeping in mind the individuality of the child at any particular age. An important aim is to help parents to change some behaviors while learning to accept others. This allows for some freedom of action for the child while giving him or her the structure, security, and acceptance of the parents.

COGNITIVE THERAPY

The origins of cognitive therapy began with Albert Ellis (1962), founder of Rational Emotive Therapy (RET), and Aaron Beck (1967). Following the rationale of cognitive therapy, it is believed that there are irrational or distorted ideas/ thoughts about oneself and the world. When working with a depressed and/or suicidal youth there are three major elements that need to be addressed:

1. Negative self-esteem
2. Negative interpretation of events
3. Negative appraisals of the future

The distinguishing characteristic of using the cognitive approach with a depressed and/or suicidal youth is to teach new learning strategies that are to be practiced and applied so that changes may occur.

The therapeutic emphasis is on teaching thinking processes. There is a need to teach the youth to identify accurately his or her own emotional experiences, to be socially cognizant of other's thoughts and feelings, and to learn the significance of behavior expectations with significant people in that youth's world.

The various techniques that are used in cognitive therapy are divided into three categories: cognitive restructuring, coping skill techniques, and problem-solving techniques.

Cognitive Restructuring

These techniques focus on the individual's irrational ideas/ beliefs. Briefly, these strategies involve problem definition, problem approach, attention focusing, choosing an answer, and self-reinforcement or coping statements (Bernard and Joyce, 1984; Kendall and Braswell, 1985). In training the youth, the counselor should model the desired behavior while verbally telling what he or she is doing.

Problem definition The youth needs to recognize and identify the problem. "What am I suppose to do when I start to feel sad?"

Problem approach The youth is encouraged to think of various strategies of solving that problem. "I need to think about what I can do. I can ask myself questions and answer them. What is it that is causing me to feel sad?"

Attention focusing Think about what's happening right now. "I need to think about what I am doing right this minute. What am I thinking? Is what I'm thinking true? Is there evidence for what I'm thinking? I need to think slowly and clearly about this."

Choosing an answer Think about the choices. Which is the best and which is worst? Think about consequences of a selected choice. "If I choose this one, what will happen? Suppose I did this, what will happen?"

Statements: Self-reinforcing Self-rewarding statements made by the youth will booster the youth's thinking processes as well as eventually raising his or her self-esteem. The youth puts the self-rewarding statements into his or her own words. "McGee, you're one OK man." "I did good." "Hey, I can do this."

Statements: Coping Encourage the youth to make an attempt at problem solving. It is the effort and the process that need to be encouraged; the answer does not always have to be correct. Change negative self-thoughts, such as "I'm dumb for thinking (choosing) that answer" to "I flubbed it," "I made a mistake," or "Guess I'll have to start thinking again."

Stress inoculation This is one aspect of cognitive restructing. An unpleasant event or situation becomes less stressful as it is incorporated as part of a person's cognitive plan. There are several stages in stress inoculation training; Meichenbaum (1975) has employed a self-instructional method.

1. *Education* Provide information or knowledge regarding the stress or crisis event. This reduces the anxiety that results from the unknown.
2. *Skill acquisition* In this stage, there are four steps: preparing for a stressor, confronting a stressor, coping with feelings of being overwhelmed, and reinforcing self-statements. Aid the youth in developing techniques for coping. Learning to cope with stress can involve identifying a stressor, utilizing relaxation techniques, roleplaying a stressful situation while trying out various alternatives, having an escape plan, and thinking positive self-statements.
3. *Application training* Role-playing with the therapist provides needed practice in trying out new coping skills.

Working out coping strategies removes passive endurance, discourages learned helplessness, and places responsibility on the youth. When a person becomes actively involved with solving his or her problems, the encouragement that is generated from within is immeasurable. Anxiety that has been caused by the stress is reduced through this active participation.

Coping Skill Techniques

These techniques focus on the development of coping skills.

Thought stopping This involves stopping an irrational belief before anxiety or discomfort begins. The youth is taught to interrupt the "bad" thoughts by snapping a rubber band that is worn around the wrist (or some other covert activity). Following this interruption, the youth is taught to take a deep breath and think about a previously selected thought or image.

Bridging or action substitution In bridging (Jewett, 1982), the youth decides which behavior is not appropriate and selects a substitute behavior for it. Usually a behavior cannot be stopped immediately, no matter how much the youth wants to stop; therefore, a bridge behavior is decided upon. This behavior is to interrupt or be a substitute for the undesirable behavior. For example, a youth who has difficulty with impulsive striking out can substitute banging his or her fist into the palm of his or her hand (instead of into someone's face or stomach) and saying, "I won't let this turkey get to me." Counting to 100 works for some children, but it has been found that, initially, most children need a physical action. As the behavior becomes more under control and inner talking continues and becomes more natural, the bridging behavior is replaced. Other examples of bridging behaviors are writing in large letters an adjective for a feeling or a thought, stomping around, and crumbling tissues.

Problem-Solving Techniques

These techniques focus on providing strategies for responding to problems. Often a youth is unable to problem solve effectively because her or his thinking is faulty.

Faulty thinking that can occur in a depressed youth are exaggeration and underestimating, ignoring strengths, personalizing, black or white thinking, and overgeneralizing (Bechtel, 1985).

In exaggeration, the youth exaggerates the problem or situation. "My life is falling apart. I just can't get myself to do any work." Or there is an underestimating of his or her ability to cope. "I never do anything right." The youth typically jumps to a faulty conclusion. "My girlfriend didn't call me because I'm a jerk."

The youth also tends to ignore his or her strengths. "Sure I made a B in English, but I got a C in math." There is only the memory of the bad or negative events in one's life.

With adolescents especially, the youth believes that everyone is noticing everything he or she does. "Boy, everyone saw me trip. What a jerk I am."

The black and white thinking becomes more prevalent. "If I don't get an A, I'm no good." "If I don't say yes, he won't like me."

Examples of overgeneralizing are "Nobody likes me." "I can't do anything right."

There is a need to deal with problems in a realistic manner. But to replace these faulty thoughts with realistic ones does not mean that the youth goes to the other extreme by viewing problems through rose-colored glasses. Problem-solving techniques aid the youth in handling or coping with problems in an orderly way.

First, it is important to bring out the negative thoughts and to be aware of them. This can be done by having the youth count or keep a record of negative thoughts. Another way to increase awareness is to write the negative thoughts down. Have the child or adolescent draw four columns. In column 1, the youth writes down the situation; in column 2, how he or she responded or what he or she thought; in column 3, the response received from others, and in column 4, what he or she was feeling. By examining in black and white the thoughts and responses, one is able to pinpoint negative thinking and behaviors.

Second, the negative thoughts must be examined. Ask questions about the thoughts—are they reasonable or are they slanted by wrong perceptions? Again, it is helpful to write down the negative thoughts and then list reasons why the negative thought is not true. Often the youth is so caught up in the black and whiteness of a situation that he or she can't see a positive or reasonable explanation for a situation. When this occurs, the counselor should brainstorm alternate explanations with the child or adolescent.

The third step is to encourage action (Bechtel, 1985). An

activity calendar or schedule is a concrete way to encourage involvement. For some youths, it is best to encourage only one activity in a week, gradually increasing activities. The individual is to record how well the activity was accomplished and how he or she felt about it. Establish with the youth a scale or some other kind of marking system for rating the feelings. For example, a 1 means Bad, a 2 means So-So, 3 is OK, 4 is Good, and 5 is Super. For elementary-age children, the school's grading system is familiar and can be used easily (i.e., A, B, C, D, and F). By keeping an activity calendar or schedule, three things are accomplished: (1) the youth is able to see in a concrete way that his or her life is not as bad as the youth perceives it to be, (2) activity is encouraged, and (3) there is a record of what activities are attached to good feelings.

After areas of faulty thinking have been identified, self-instruction can be utilized for problem solving. The youth is taught to control his or her behaviors by making covert, gradually going to overt, self-suggestions. By this is meant first talking aloud about the problem, what it is, looking at the choices, and then deciding which is the best/worst choice. The youth is gradually helped to go from verbal speech, to whispers, to inner thoughts.

PEER COUNSELING

"Peer counselors can be used both in the classroom and in human-relations classes and as part of the outreach program of the counseling and guidance program of the school. Given proper training and supervision, peers can often be as effective in reaching fellow students as counselors and teachers" (Corey and Corey, 1987, p. 296).

Peer counselors are a resource often overlooked by the school. Corey and Corey (1987) make some important points in using peer counselors. It is important for peer counselors, as well as for counselors in general, to be aware of their own limitations. They can play a supportive role, as well as challenge fellow students to look at their own behaviors, and they can share their own experiences and learning with other students. More importantly, they can act as a contact or outreach person to their peers since students confide in peers more than with adults. They are not qualified to do psychotherapy and should be discouraged from trying out that role.

The goals in training peer counselors are to dispel the myths of suicide; teach listening and communication skills; facilitate the communication among students, administration, faculty, and parents; and be knowledgeable of confidentiality and referral issues.

Regardless of how peer counselors are chosen, and whatever type of training they are given, they can be a positive influence in any intervention program.

GROUP COUNSELING

Group counseling can be used to focus on depressed and low-risk suicidal youth. The group is not aimed at major personality changes but would deal with specific issues or topics on a short-term basis. The goals of group counseling would be to prevent and to remediate situational problems. The group uses an interpersonal process that stresses conscious thoughts, feelings, and behaviors. Groups can be used effectively to cope with the stresses of a situational crisis (Corey and Corey, 1987).

Thompson and Rudolph (1983) suggest four types of groups, three of which we feel are appropriate for use with depressed and low-risk suicidal youths.

1. The case-centered group consists of children working on different problems. Each child has the opportunity to receive the group's full attention to his or her problem.
2. The human-potential group provides an opportunity for children to develop their positive traits and strengths. The focus is on developmental concerns rather than remedial concerns.
3. The skill-development group is directed to specific behaviors and skills. For example, children may improve

their basic communication skills by practicing active listening.

The types and goals of groups, while differing, do retain basic common elements of counseling techniques. There is the need to establish rapport, develop trust within the group, and set goals. With younger children, the group may need to be more structured, as the children may be less verbal.

There are various techniques that can be used within the groups to facilitate the group process. Such techniques could be: drawing pictures of animals, answering "what if . . ." questions, employing values clarification, keeping a "Feelings" or a "Me" journal, playing various card games such as "Old Maid" or "War," listing five things they like/dislike about school (or self), saying one positive word or adjective about another group member, listing three ways to be dependent/ independent, and sharing two scary (mad, happy) feelings. These techniques are not all-inclusive but are presented as examples of what can be done within a group.

SUMMARY

It is appropriate and important that the school take some initiative or responsibility in dealing with the feelings and emotions of children and adolescents following a suicide or sudden death. Although some professionals within the public schools are voicing some concern regarding an overemphasis and overreaction to suicide, it is felt that this concern is more of a personal nature in that it imposes more time, responsibility, and effort than these individuals are willing to give. Their feeling is that it takes away from their main responsibility of teaching. But is not the teaching of self-reliance and adjustment to new and stressful situations part of the learning process? And is the death of a student so unimportant that it be preempted by educational goals? Insensitivity to the emotional needs of students is something we can ill afford to have in our teachers. Fortunately, the majority of educators are fully aware of, interested in, and concerned about all aspects of their students' learning and adjustment.

Recommended Books

Cognitive-Behavioral Therapy for Impulsive Children by Kendall and Braswell (1985).

Cognitive Therapy of Depression by Beck, Rush, Shaw, and Emery (1979).

Counseling Children by Thompson and Rudolph (1983).

Groups: Process and Practice by Corey and Corey (1987).

Helping Children Cope with Separation and Loss by Jewett (1982).

Rational-Emotive Therapy with Children and Adolescents by Bernard and Joyce (1984).

Teaching Social Skills to Children by Cartledge and Milburn (1986).

100 Ways to Enhance Self-Concept in the Classroom by Canfield and Wells (1976).

References

Abramson, L. Y.; Seligman, M. E. P.; and Teasdale, J. D. 1978. Learned helplessness in humans: Critique and reformulation. *Journal of Abnormal Psychology* 87: 49–74.

Ackerly, W. C. 1967. Latency-age children who threaten or attempt to kill themselves. *Journal American Academy Child Psychiatry* 6: 242–261.

Allen, N. H., and Peck, M. 1977. *Suicide in young people.* West Point, Penn.: American Association of Suicidology. Merck, Sharp and Dohme, Division of Merck and Co., Inc.

American Psychiatric Association. 1980. *Diagnostic and statistical manual of mental disorders.* 3rd ed. Washington, D.C.

American Psychiatric Association. 1984. *Psychiatric glossary.* 5th ed. Washington, D.C.

Anthony, E. J. 1975. Childhood depression. In E. J. Anthony and T. Benedek (Eds.), *Depression and human existence.* Boston: Little, Brown.

Arnold, A. 1972. *A world book of children's games.* New York: T. Y. Crowell.

Bandura, A. 1969. *Principles of behavior modification.* New York: Holt, Rinehart and Winston.

Barman, A. 1976. *Helping children face crisis.* Public Affairs Pamphlet #541. New York: Public Affairs Committee, pp. 8–9.

Baron, C. March 1986. Child welfare league conference looks at teen suicides in group care. *Network News,* 4–5.

Bask, M. A. S., and Camp, B. W. 1986. In G. Cartledge and J. A. F. Milburn (Eds.), *Teaching social skills to children.* New York: Pergamon Press.

Bechtel, S. March 1985. Self-talk: New way to beat the blues. *Prevention,* 141–146.

Beck, A. T. 1967. *Depression: Causes and treatment.* Philadelphia: University of Pennsylvania Press.

Beck, A. T.; Rush, A. J.; Shaw, B. E.; and Emery, G. 1979. *Cognitive therapy of depression.* New York: Guilford Press.

Bender, L., and Schilder, P. 1937. Suicidal preoccupation and attempts in children. *American Journal of Orthopsychiatry* 7: 225–235.

Benson, H. 1975. *The relaxation response.* New York: Wm. Morrow and Co.

Berkovitz, I. H. 1985. The role of schools in child, adolescent, and youth suicide prevention. In M. L. Peck, N. L. Farberow, and R. E. Litman (Eds.), *Youth suicide.* New York: Springer, pp. 170–190.

Bernard, M. E., and Joyce, M. R. 1984. *Rational-emotive therapy with children and adolescents: Theory, treatment strategies, preventative methods.* New York: John Wiley & Sons.

Bloomquist, K. R. 1974. Nurse, I need help—The school nurse's role in suicide prevention. *Journal of Psychiatric Nursing and Mental Health Services* 1: 22–26.

Blumenthal, S., and Hirschfeld, R. 1984. Suicide among adolescents and young adults. National Institute of Mental Health. Washington, D.C.: U.S. Government Printing Office.

Bowen, M. 1978. *Family therapy in clinical practice.* New York: Jason Aronson.

Bowlby, J. 1960. Grief and mourning in infancy and early childhood. *Psychoanalytic Study of the Child* 15: 9–15.

Brown, S. L. 1985. Adolescents and family systems. In M. L. Peck, N. L. Farberow, and R. E. Litman (Eds.), *Youth suicide.* New York: Springer, pp. 71–79.

Canfield, J., and Wells, H. C. 1976. *100 ways to enhance self-concept in the classroom.* Englewood Cliffs, N.J.: Prentice-Hall.

Cartledge, G., and Milburn, J. F. 1986. *Teaching social skills to children.* 2nd ed. New York: Pergamon Press.

Center for Disease Control. March 1985. *Suicide surveillance report, Summary: 1970–1980.* Atlanta, Ga.: U. S. Department of Health and Human Services. Public Health Service.

Center for Disease Control. November 1986. *Suicide surveillance report, Summary: 1970–1980.* Atlanta, Ga.: U.S. Department of Health and Human Services. Public Health Service.

Chapman, A. H. 1974. *Management of emotional problems of children and adolescents.* 2nd ed. Philadelphia: Lippincott.

Clarizio, H. 1982. Childhood depression: Diagnosis considerations. *Psychology in the Schools* 181–197.

Cohen-Sandler, R., and Berman, A. 1980. Diagnosis and treatment of childhood depression and self-destructive behavior. *Journal Family Practice* 11: 51–58.

Cohen-Sandler, R., and Berman, A. 1982. Life stress and symptomatology: Determinants of suicidal behavior in children. *Journal American Academy of Child Psychiatry* 21, 2: 178–186.

Cohen-Sandler, R.; Berman, A.; and King, R. 1982. A follow-up study of hospitalized suicidal children. *Journal of the American Academy of Child Psychiatry* 21, 4: 398–403.

Coleman, L. March 1986. Teen suicide clusters and the Werther Effect. *Network News,* 1, 6, 7, 8.

Coleman, L. 1987. *Clusters.* Boston: Faber and Faber.

Corey, G. 1977. *Theory and practice and counseling and psychotherapy.* Oakland, Calif.: Brooks/Cole.

Corey, M. S., and Corey, G. 1987. *Groups: Process and practice.* Monterey, Calif.: Brooks/Cole.

Crumley, F. E. 1982. The adolescent suicide attempt: A cardinal symptom of a serious psychiatric disorder. *American Journal of Psychotherapy* 34: 2.

Dorpat, I.; Jackson, J. K.; and Ripley, M. S. 1965. Broken homes and attempted and completed suicides. *Archives of General Psychiatry* 12: 213–216.

Ellis, A. 1962. *Reason and emotion in psychotherapy.* New York: Lyle Stuart.

Emde, R. N.; Harmon, R. J.; and Good, W. V. 1986. Depressive feeling in children: A transactional model for research. In M. Rutter, C. E. Izard, and P. B. Read (Eds.), *Depression in young people: Clinical and developmental perspectives.* New York: Guilford Press, pp. 135–160.

Finch, S., and Poznanski, E. 1971. *Adolescent suicide.* Springfield, Ill.: Charles C. Thomas.

Friedman, R. C.; Corn, R.; Hurt, S.; Fibel, B.; Schulick, J.; and Swirsky, S. (1984). Family history of illness in the seriously suicidal adolescent: A life-cycle approach. *American Journal of Orthopsychiatry* 54, 3: 390–397.

Garfinkel, B. D. 1986. School based prevention programs. Paper presented at the National Conference on Prevention and Intervention in Youth Suicide, June 1986, Oakland, Calif.

Garfinkel, B.; Froese, A.; and Hood, J. 1982. Suicide attempts in children and adolescents. *American Journal of Psychiatry* 139: 10.

Garfinkel, B., and Golombek, H. 1974. Suicide and depression in childhood and adolescence. *Canadian Medical Association Journal* 110: 1278–1281.

Giffin, M., and Felsenthal, C. 1983. *A cry for help.* New York: Doubleday and Co.

Gilead, M., and Mulaik, J. 1983. Adolescent suicide: A response to developmental crisis. *Perspectives in Psychiatric Care* 14, 3: 94–101.

Gispert, M.; Davis, M. S.; Marsh, L.; and Wheeler, K. April 1967. Preventive factors in repeated suicide attempts in adolescents. *Hospital and Community Psychiatry.*

Glaser, D. 1978. The treatment of depressed and suicidal adolescents. *American Journal of Psychotherapy* 23: 252–269.

Glaser, K. 1965. Attempted suicide in children and adolescents: Psychodynamic observations. *American Journal of Psychotherapy* 19: 220–227.

Glaser, K. 1968. Masked depression in children and adolescents. *Annual Progress in Child Psychiatry and Child Development* 1: 345–355.

Good, T., and Brophy, J. 1978. *Looking in classrooms.* New York: Harper and Row.

Gordon, T. 1975. *Parent effectiveness training.* New York: The New American Library.

Gould, R. E. 1965. Suicide problems in children and adolescents. *American Journal Psychotherapy* 19: 228–246.

Grollman, E. A. 1971. *Suicide (Prevention, intervention, postvention).* Boston: Beacon Press.

Harrison, M. 1976. *For the fun of it: Selected cooperative games for children and adults.* Philadelphia: Nonviolence and Children Series. Friends Peace Committee.

Hatton, C. L., and Valente, S. McB. 1984. *Suicide assessment and intervention.* Norwalk, Conn.: Appleton-Century-Crofts.

Hipple, J., and Cimbolic, P. 1979. *The counselor and suicidal crisis.* Springfield, Ill.: Charles C. Thomas.

Howe, L. W., and Howe, M. M. 1975. *Personalizing education—Values clarification and beyond.* New York: Hart.

Humphrey, J. H., and Humphrey, J. N. 1985. *Controlling stress in children.* Springfield, Ill.: Charles C. Thomas.

Jacobs, J., and Teicher, J. 1969. Broken homes and social isolation in attempted suicides of adolescents. *International Journal of Social Psychiatry* 13: 139–149.

Jewett, C. 1982. *Helping children cope with separation and loss.* Harvard, Ma.: Harvard Common Press.

Johns, B., and Johns, M. October 1983. Stress burns out kids, too. *Education Digest* 49: 44–46.

Kanfer, F., and Goldstein, A. P. 1975. *Helping people change: A textbook of methods.* New York: Pergamon Press.

Kaslow, N. J., and Rehm, L. P. 1983. Childhood depression. In R. J. Morris and T. R. Kratochwill (Eds.), *The practice of child therapy.* New York: Pergamon Press.

Kastenbaum, R. 1959. Time and death in adolescence. In Herman Feifel (Ed.), *In the meaning of death.* New York: Mc-Graw-Hill, pp. 99–113.

Kendall, R. C., and Braswell, L. 1985. *Cognitive-behavioral therapy for impulsive children.* New York: Guilford Press.

Klagsbrun, F. 1981. *Too young to die.* New York: Pocket Books.

Knapp, S., and Vandesreek, L. 1982. Tarasoff: Five years later. *Professional Psychology* 13: 511–516.

Kovacs, M., and Beck, A. T. 1977. An empirical-clinical approach toward a definition of childhood depression. In J. G. Schulterbradt and A. Raskin (Eds.), *Depression in childhood: Diagnostic, treatment and conceptual models.* New York: Raven Press.

Lederman, J. 1973. *Anger and the rocking chair.* New York: Viking Press.

Levenson, M. 1984. Cognitive correlated of suicidal risk. In C. Neuringer (Ed.), *Psychological assessment of suicidal risk.* Chicago: Charles C Thomas.

Levenson, M., and Neuringer, C. 1971. Problem-solving behavior in suicidal adolescents. *Journal of Consulting and Clinical Psychology* 37, 3: 433–436.

Lourie, R. S. 1967. Suicide and attempted suicide in children and adolescents. *Texas Medicine* 63: 58–63.

Lukianowicz, N. 1968. Attempted suicide in children. *Acta Psychitrica Scandinavica* 44: 416–435.

Mattson, A.; Seese, L. R.; and Hawkins, J. W. 1969. Suicidal behavior as a child psychiatric emergency. *Archives of General Psychiatry* 20: 100–109.

McAnarney, E. 1979. Adolescent and young adult suicide in the United States—A reflection of societal unrest? *Adolescent* 14: 765–774.

McCaffrey, I. December 1974. Elementary school children with persistent emotional disturbances. State Department of Mental Hygiene, Albany, New York.

McCoy, K. 1982. *Coping with teenage depression: A parent's guide.* New York: New American Library.

McIntire, M. S.; Angle, C. R.; and Struempler, L. J. 1972. The concept of death in midwestern children and youth. *American Journal of Diseases of Children* 123: 527–532.

McNamee, A. S., and McNamee, J. E. 1981. Stressful life experiences in the early childhood educational setting. In C. R. Wells and I. R. Stuart (Eds.), *Self-destructive behavior in children and adolescents.* New York: Van Nostrand Reinhold.

Meichenbaum, D. 1975. A self-instructional approach to stress inoculation training. In I. Sarason and C. D. Spielberger (Eds.), *Stress and anxiety.* New York: Wiley & Sons.

Morrison, G. C., and Collier, J. G. 1969. Family treatment approaches to suicidal children and adolescents. *Journal of American Academy of Child Psychiatry* 8: 140–153.

Nagy, M. 1959. The child's view of death. In H. Feidel (Ed.), *The meaning of death.* New York: McGraw-Hill.

Nelson, E. R., and Slaikeu, K. A. 1984. Crisis intervention in the schools. In K. A. Slaikeu (Ed.), *Crisis intervention: A handbook for practice and research.* Boston: Allyn and Bacon.

New Haven Register. January 1987. Father of teen suicide victim sues school officials. Pp. 1–2.

Orbach, I.; Gross, Y.; and Glaubman, H. 1981. Some common characteristics of latency-age suicidal children: A tentative model based on case study analyses. *Suicide and Life-Threatening Behavior* 11: 3.

Orlick, T. 1978. *The cooperative sports and games book: Challenge without competition.* New York: Pantheon Books.

Otte, D., and DeBlassie, R. 1985. Bereaved children. *Pastoral Life,* July-August: 2–7.

Pattison, E. M. 1977. *The experience of dying.* Englewood Cliffs, N. J.: Prentice-Hall.

Patsiokas, A. T.; Clum, G. A.; and Luscomb, R. L. 1979. Cognitive characteristics of suicide attempters. *Journal of Consulting and Clinical Psychology* 3: 478–484.

Pearce, J. 1977. Depressive disorders in childhood. *Journal of Child Psychology and Psychiatry* 18: 79–83.

Peck, M. 1982. Youth suicide. *Death Education* 6: 29–47.

Pfeffer, C. R. 1981a. The family system of suicidal children. *American Journal of Psychotherapy* 35: 330–341.

Pfeffer, C. R. 1981b. The distinctive features of children who threaten and attempt suicide. In C. R. Wells and I. R. Stuart (Eds.), *Self-destructive behavior in children and adolescents.* New York: Van Nostrand Reinhold.

Pfeffer, C. R.; Conte, H. R.; Plutchik, R.; and Jerrett, I. 1979. Suicidal behavior in latency age children. *Journal American Academy of Child Psychiatry* 18: 679–692.

Phillips, D. P. 1974. The influence of suggestion on suicide: Substantive and theoretical implications of the Werther effect. *American Sociologist Review* 39: 340–354.

Phillips, D. P., and Carstensen, L. L. 1986. The clustering of teenage suicides after television news stories about suicide. *The New England Journal of Medicine* 315, 11: 685–689.

Piaget, J. 1923. *Language and thought of the child.* London: Routledge and Kegan.

Raths, L.; Harmin, M.; and Simon, S. B. 1964. *Values and teaching.* Columbus, Ohio: Merrill.

Ray, L., and Johnson, N. November 1983. Adolescent suicide. *The Personnel and Guidance Journal,* 131–135.

Reed, S. May 1984. Stress what makes kids vulnerable? *Instructor,* 28–31.

Ringness, T. A. 1975. *The affective domain in education.* Boston: Brown and Co.

Robbins, D. R., and Alessi, N. E. 1985. Depressive symptoms and suicidal behavior in adolescents. *American Journal of Psychiatry* 142, 5: 588–592.

Rochlin, G. 1959. The loss complex. *Journal American Psychoanalytic Association* 7: 299–309.

Rosenthal, P. A., and Rosenthal, S. 1984. Suicidal behavior by preschool children. *American Journal of Psychiatry* 141, 4: 520–525.

Ross, C. P. 1985. Teaching children the facts of life and death: Suicide prevention in the schools. In M. L. Peck, N. L. Farberow, and R. E. Litman (Eds.), *Youth suicide.* New York: Springer.

Sabbath, J. C. 1969. The suicidal adolescent—The expendable child. *Journal American Academy Child Psychiatry* 8: 272–289.

Schaefer, C. E., and Millman, H. L. 1981. *How to help children with common problems.* New York: Litter Educational Publishing.

Select Committee on Aging, House of Representatives. 1985. *Suicide and suicide prevention* (Comm. Pub. No. 98–497). Washington, D.C.: U.S. Government Printing Office.

Seligman, M. E. P. 1975. *Helplessness: On depression, development and death.* San Francisco: Freeman.

Shaffer, D. 1974. Suicide in childhood and early adolescence. *Journal of Child Psychiatry* 15: 275–291.

Shafii, M.; Carrigan, S.; Whittinghill, J. R.; and Derrick, A. 1985. Psychological autopsy of completed suicide in children and adolescents. *American Journal of Psychiatry* 142: 1061–1063.

Shamoo, T. K., and Patros, P. G. 1985. Suicide intervention strategies for the adolescent. *Techniques: A Journal for Remedial Education and Counseling* 1, 4: 297–303.

Shaw, C. R., and Schelkin, R. F. 1965. Suicidal behavior in children. *Psychiatry* 28: 157–168.

Sheperd, M.; Oppenheim, B.; and Mitchell, S. 1971. *Childhood behavior and mental health.* New York: Grune and Stratton.

Shneidman, E. March 1987. At the point of no return. *Psychology Today* 21, 3: 54–58.

Slaikeu, K. A. 1984. *Crisis intervention: A handbook for practice and research.* Boston: Allyn and Bacon.

Spitz, R. 1946. Anaclitic depression. *Psychoanalytic Study of the Child* 2: 313–342.

Stanley, E. S., and Barter, J. T. 1970. Adolescent suicidal behavior. *American Journal Orthopsychiatry* 40: 87–96.

Thompson, C., and Rudolph, L. 1983. *Counseling children.* Monterey, Calif.: Brooks/Cole.

Teicher, J. D., and Jacobs, J. 1966. Adolescents who attempt suicide: Preliminary findings. *American Journal of Psychiatry* 122: 1248–1257.

Turkington, C. 1983. Child suicide: An unspoken tragedy. *American Psychological Association Monitor* 14: 15.

Wells, C. R., and Stuart, I. R. 1981. *Self-destructive behavior in children and adolescents.* New York: Van Nostrand Reinhold.

World Book Encyclopedia. 1981. s.v. "Death." Chicago: *Child-craft International* 5, 52–53.

Index